D1325201

Lyke Wake Walk

£1.50

Lyke Wake Walk

Forty Miles across the
North York Moors

by

Bill Cowley

DALESMAN BOOKS
1979

The Dalesman Publishing Company Ltd.
Clapham (via Lancaster), North Yorkshire

First published 1959
Eighth edition 1979

© Bill Cowley, 1959, 1979

ISBN: 0 85206 501 9

Printed and Bound in Great Britain by
Galava Printing Co. Ltd., Hallam Road, Nelson, Lancashire.

Contents

*Acknowledgements are due to various members of the Club for
photographs which appear on pages 49-56
and to A.E.F. Wright for the maps.*

Cover photo: Scarth Wood Moor, looking east, by Bill Cowley.

Maps on pages 23-26.

*NOTE: Large sections of the Lyke Wake Walk are accepted rights of
way; others by agreement with landowners. Nothing in the
text should be taken as implying a legal right of way, but no
objections have been made to date on the routes indicated.*

When You are on the Moors

THE art of moorland walking is always to look well ahead and pick a route that will take advantage of sheep tracks, short heather, and burnt patches or "swiddens". On a well-cared-for moor, the heather is never allowed to grow too long but patches are burned in rotation, young heather shoots being a favourite food of both grouse and sheep.

It is better to detour a little than to plough through deep heather on a compass course, and it will cause far less disturbance to grouse in the nesting season. Parties should walk in single file and be as quiet as possible. Spreading out and shouting, particularly at night, with lights, can scare sheep into running to their deaths in a bog. A solemn silence should always prevail on the Lyke Wake Walk. Keep dogs on a lead.

Give shooting parties a very wide berth in your own interest as well as theirs. It is important always to be careful where you go and how you go, and to retain the friendship of all concerned. Please never leave litter of any kind unless it is well buried. A tin can lame a sheep, a bottle can start a fire.

Remember—this is a tough walk. In really bad winter conditions it can be impossible. Never tackle it unless fully trained and prepared. Don't be afraid to turn back. Never go on to Wheeldale or Fylingdale Moors alone if already exhausted. Think of others—and do not expect a welcome at any farm or inn at unreasonable hours.

In thick mist be careful on Carlton and Cringle Moors. Watch out for rock outcrops, and for high embankments along the old railway.

SEVEN POINTS ON SAFETY

The greatest danger on the North Yorkshire Moors lies in sudden changes of weather. You can have sunshine in the morning and hailstones in the afternoon. A light drizzle in the valley may be a blizzard on the moor-top. Therefore *remember*:

1. Always take map and compass (and make sure you can use them).
2. Carry a wind-proof anorak and spare warm clothing even in summer. Wear boots.
3. Pack a torch, a reserve of food, a small first-aid kit, and a *whistle* (which in emergency carries further and lasts longer than the human voice).
4. Always leave word of your route, and stick to it. Make sure *someone* knows where you have gone. Have a central phone number to report to if you give up, or inform the police so that time is not wasted looking for you.
5. A safe number for a party is five. If anyone is hurt two can stay with him and two go for help.
6. Study the map, and note the quickest and safest ways to get off the moors, and the nearest telephones.
7. If hopelessly lost at night, shelter in deep heather, out of the wind, eat some of your emergency food, and wait for daylight. Put all spare clothing on immediately you stop, *before* you begin to get cold. And stop *before* you are exhausted. In an emergency, inform the police as soon as possible.

ROUTE PLANNING

For a summer daylight crossing it is best to start at 4 a.m. after a night's sleep and walk straight through to finish by 10 p.m. For a party not too fit a good way is to start at 6 p.m., sleep at Clay Bank 10 p.m. to 4 a.m. and finish at 6 p.m. again. Keep a rough time schedule for each section. Restrict rest stops to 15 mins. or at most 30 mins. Leave some agreed sign at crossing points if you decide to go on before your support party arrives (e.g. an arrow of small stones indicating a note — *not* indiscriminate chalk marks, please).

EQUIPMENT

Footwear — Walking shoes or gym shoes are not suitable for moorland walking. *Always* wear boots. These need not be expensive, but they must be strong and large enough to wear with *two* pairs of socks. Soft fell boots are best. In dry summer conditions basketball boots may be useful.

Clothing — Always wear (or carry) long trousers, preferably made of wool or cord. Jeans are most unsuitable as they retain little warmth and corduroys are difficult to dry. An anorak or wind-cheater is essential. This should be as windproof and as waterproof as possible, whilst avoiding condensation on the inside. Rubber materials are unsuitable.

7

A plastic mackintosh or a waterproof cover made from one of the new proofed materials is the best protection against heavy rain. Carry spare emergency clothing; if the weather should deteriorate it will save you a lot of discomfort and hardship.

HEATHER BIVOUACS

Even in winter a night on the moors need not be disastrous. If near a valley, go down into it to the first bracken, and make a deep nest of bracken and heather, pulling plenty on top of you. On the moor itself find a patch of deep heather and a sheltered hollow. Use loose stones to build a wind-break. Pull enough heather to make a bed below and a blanket on top.

Cleveland Lyke Wake Dirge

This yah neet, this yah neet,
   Ivvery neet an' all,
Fire an' fleet an' cannle leet,
   An' Christ tak up thy saul.
When thoo frae hence away art passed
   Ivvery neet an' all,
Ti Whinny Moor thoo cums at last,
   An' Christ tak up thy saul.
If ivver thoo gav owther hosen or shoon,
   Ivvery neet an' all,
Clap thee doon, an' put 'em on,
   An' Christ tak up thy saul.
Bud if hosen an' shoon thoo nivver gav neean,
   Ivvery neet an' all,
T'whinnies'll prick thee sair ti t'beean,
   An' Christ tak up thy saul.
Frae Whinny Moor when thoo art passed
   Ivvery neet an' all,
Ti t'Brig o' Dreead thoo cums at last,
   An' Christ tak up thy saul.
If ivver thoo gav o' thy siller an' gowd,
   Ivvery neet an' all,
On t'Brig o' Dreead thoo'll finnd footho'd,
   An' Christ tak up thy saul.
Bud if siller an' gowd thoo nivver gav neean,
   Ivvery neet an' all.
Thoo'll doon, doon tum'le towards Hell fleeame,
   An' Christ tak up thy saul.
Frae t'Brig o' Dreead when thoo art passed
   Ivvery neet an' all,
Ti t'fleeames o' Hell thoo'll cum at last,
   An' Christ tak up thy saul.
If ivver thoo gav owther bite or sup,
   Ivvery neet an' all,
T' fleeames'll nivver catch thee up,
   An' Christ tak up thy saul.
Bud if bite or sup thoo nivver gav neean,
   Ivvery neet an' all,
T' flames'll bon thee sair ti t'beean,
   An' Christ tak up thy saul.

fleet—flame; **neean**—none; **beean**—bone; **bon**—burn.
(Richard Blakeborough's version, with amendments)

THIS Dirge is probably our oldest dialect verse. John Aubrey wrote in 1686 "The beliefe in Yorkshire was amongst the vulgar (perhaps is in part still) that after the person's death the soule went over Whinny-Moore, and till about 1616-24 at the funerale a woman came and sang the following song." Richard Blakeborough records that it was last sung at a funeral near Kildale about 1800. The Dirge was known widely in the North — Sir Walter Scott had a version — but the Cleveland form seems more authentic. "Wake" means the watching over a corpse, and "Lyke" is the corpse itself — as in the "lych" gate of a church — c/f. German *"leich"*.

Canon Atkinson, of Danby, believed that "fleet" was a variant of "flet", a Cleveland term for live coals or embers. "The usage was on no account to suffer the fire in the house to go out during the time the corpse was in it, and throughout the same time a candle was invariably kept burning in the room."

The ideas in the Dirge go back to the earliest Norse and, indeed, general Aryan folk lore — perhaps even to the Bronze Age people who burned and buried their dead on the high points of our moors, where their grave-mounds are now our guiding marks. Apart from this there is no suggestion that corpses were carried over the Lyke Wake Walk, and the connection between Walk and Dirge is merely that members of the first party to do the Walk, like many who have done it since, finding themselves in the middle of Wheeldale Moor at 3 a.m. felt a great sympathy with all the souls who have to do such a crossing, and a real affection for the poetry of the Dirge — its stark simplicity, repetitions, and dramatic power.

Perhaps only those who have crossed Wheeldale or Fylingdales Moors with storm and darkness threatening can fully appreciate the beauty of the Lyke Wake Dirge.

How this Moorland Walk Began

FOR me, as for anyone born on Tees-side or on the Cleveland Plain, the Cleveland Hills were the backcloth of boyhood. I spent days tramping the high moors, sleeping in the heather or at a friendly farm. The nearest I ever got to the present Lyke Wake Walk was a walk from Danby to Troutsdale and back through Farndale to Broughton, in three days.

On returning from India in 1947 I bought a 21-acre smallholding at Over Silton, below Black Hambleton, and wrote in *The Dalesman* then that from the moor gate at the top of the village a man could walk for three days through the heather, to the sea near Whitby, and never meet a soul. And if he did it in August or September he would kick up a cloud of purple pollen at every step for forty miles.

This thought occurred to me again in August, 1955, when I had an interest in Glaisdale Head Farm. One evening I climbed up alone on to the rigg between Glaisdale and Fryupdale. To the north and east the sea lay in a great blue arc beyond Danby and Lealholm Moors. But to the south lay mystery and romance; for there the dimensions were of time as well as space. The moors undulated endlessly, dotted with tumuli, and I began to imagine them peopled with ghosts of a remote past — little men with stone axes or flint arrows, coming to the edge of the moor and looking down into valleys thick with forest or full of marsh and lake.

> *Grey recumbent tombs of the dead in desert places,*
> *Standing stones on the vacant wine-red moor,*
> *Hills of sheep, and the homes of the silent vanquished races,*
> *And winds austere and pure.*

And I wrote again then in *The Dalesman* that this was one of the wildest stretches of moor in Yorkshire; that you could get on to the "tops" above Swainby and walk due east on heather all the way, except for crossing one or two roads; that you would cross round the head of Scugdale to Chop Yat, Botton Head and Bloworth, after which Flat Howe, Loose Howe and Shunner Howe would bring you

11

to Glaisdale Head in about twenty miles of tough walking. But (I wrote enthusiastically, not knowing what I was letting myself in for) you could keep on across open moor, keeping south of Wheeldale Gill, over How Moor and Simon Howe, by Tom Cross Rigg and Snod Hill to Lilla Howe, then over Fylingdales Moor to the sea. The heather would provide a luxurious bed, and you might never meet a soul for the two or three days it might take you.

At this point, a little carried away by my own eloquence, I issued a challenge to anyone to get from Scarth Wood Moor above Mount Grace Priory, the most westerly point of the range, to Wyke Point at Ravenscar, the most easterly in 24 hours on his own feet. Four months later, again in *The Dalesman*, I was describing the first successful crossing:

There was no question of racing. We meant to enjoy the walk. But we knew it would be a tough test—a minor Everest of our own making. We had all lived with maps in hand or mind for days, weighing alternative routes. Now came the final choice—and the weather was perfect.

We took the alum miner's track round the face of Carlton Moor, Cringle Moor and Cold Moor, with the Cleveland Plain spread out below in a gigantic patchwork quilt of pasture and stubble fields stretching away to the Pennines by Cross Fell, or across smoky Teesside to the Durham hills. Four of us reached Clay Bank Top in 2½ hours, glad of the mobile bar that awaited us!

We reached the high point of Botton Head (1,489 ft.) right on schedule at 3.30 p.m. Now we were deep in the moors and deep in heather. All our concentration was required to find the easiest and shortest way through, a Bronze Age mound or a leaning stone our guide, to the Smugglers' Trod, its stone flags now heaved crazily about by heather roots. Darkness was just closing in on us as we saw the lights and tents of our bivouac round the ruined inn of Hamer. The Cleveland Lyke Wake Dirge came to our minds:

> *This yah neet, this yah neet,*
> *Ivvery neet an' all,*
> *Fire an' fleet an' cannle leet,*
> *An' Christ tak up thy saul.*

We gave a great shout and rushed down through the heather. We had covered 21 miles in seven hours and had earned a rest. Few of us got much sleep. The worst part still lay ahead. The real testing time of this walk started at 3.30 a.m. Before us was the wild stretch of Wheeldale Moor, with never a track across it. Just four miles of knee-deep heather till we reached the Roman highway at the other side.

The moon was veiled by clouds. The light and the contours were most deceitful. We felt rather than saw the sudden drop into Wheeldale Gill, our guide to the left. To the right was only the cold night wind on our cheeks. Startled grouse kept exploding from the heather at our feet and grumbling away into the darkness. Shallow dips seemed like deep valleys, and sometimes we fell full length in an unseen hole.

> 'Twere a dree neet, a dree neet, ower Whinny Moor ti trake,
> Wi' shoonless feet, ower flinty steeans, thruff monny a thorny brake;
> A dree neet, a dree neet, wi' nowt neeaways ti mark
> T'gainest trod ti t'Brig o' Dreead, a lane lost sowl i' t' dark.

We kept checking our course by compass, slightly south of east. One solitary light in Goathland gave us another check, then suddenly an intake wall loomed ahead by the Stape road. Beyond was Wade's Causeway and the steep track down to a dark and silent Wheeldale Lodge. At 5.30 a.m. we were sitting on the stepping stones chewing chocolate, the wide stream a subdued silver between rustling trees. There was another hard climb through rocks and bracken on to Howl Moor. Dawn broke slowly as we approached the railway cutting at Ellerbeck. We crossed by Fen House, over Tom Cross Rigg to the Whitby road. A rest and a cold breakfast, and we set off along the Salt track for Lilla Howe.

It was 10 a.m. as we crossed the Scarborough road near Helwath Bridge and knew we were well inside the time. Even so, the last rough patches of heather over Pye Rigg Howe were a sore trial, and it was with weary limbs and sore heels, but glad hearts, that we tramped into Ravenscar at last down the road from the old windmill. Blue sea and golden sands were just beginning to show through the mist as the sun gained strength, and the cliffs beyond the bay took shape as we celebrated our triumph with the Goulton Tankard and formed the Lyke Wake Club.

★　　★　　★

The times on the first walk were: 12 noon, leave Triangulation Pillar; 2.30, arrive Clay Bank Top; 2.55, leave Clay Bank Top; 3.30, Botton Head; 5.0, arrive Blakey Rigg; 5.30, leave Blakey Rigg; 7.0, arrive Hamer; 3.30 a.m., leave Hamer; 5.30, Wheeldale Lodge; 7.25, arrive Tom Cross Rigg; 8.00, leave Tom Cross Rigg; 11 a.m., arrive Ravenscar.

[13 hours actual walking time].

IN the last five years the Lyke Wake Walk has — quite unofficially — become a national institution. It has not been recognised by any National Park or local authority. It has certainly never received any official help or encouragement from any source. But nearly 80,000 people have now done at least one crossing, and crossings are currently at the rate of over 9,000 a year. There were over 3,000 crossings in June 1978 alone. The Lyke Wake Walk is marked on the 1-inch Ordnance Survey Map, North York Moors, new edition (1967), because it exists now as a well-marked track on the ground.

This is a great change from 15 years ago, when for most of the way the walk was over heather with no tracks at all and it was unusual to meet anyone along the route. Part of the original challenge has therefore gone, but in bad conditions (which are very frequent) the walk can still be an adventure and parties still get lost. There is always danger on the hills, but only in bad weather conditions is anyone likely to take any real harm from being lost on the Lyke Wake Walk.

Solitude can be found elsewhere on the moors, and the weekend parties who meet each other on the Lyke Wake Walk share instead a pleasant comradeship, an exchange of comment and advice. Lyke Wake Walkers are peculiar only in the sense that they appreciate the beauty of the moors in a way that no one else can who has not walked 40 miles across them in 24 hours, and in that they have the confidence of achievement and of real physical fitness. Otherwise they are a cross-section of the community and include two Chief Constables, many policemen and policewomen, four Group Captains, one Air Vice-Marshal and several Colonels, members of Civil Defence and the Fire Services, students from most universities (and from several Approved Schools), industrial apprentices, doctors, dentists and engineers, French, Norwegians, Danes, Germans, Americans, Australians, Indians and Africans.

The Lyke Wake Club provides over a quarter of the 80 National Park Voluntary Wardens, and the greater part of the Cleveland Moors Search and Rescue Team. In this way and through its circulars the Club does a great deal to educate young walkers in correct behaviour on the moors. Certainly the main danger to the moors lies not in walkers, whatever their number, but in the many encroachments that continue to be made. In the last 15 years more natural moorland has been spoiled than in the previous 4,000 years.

Whatever may be the economic benefit involved, every new threat of interference by gas, oil, TV masts or improvement of roads (other than the main ones) must be resisted strongly. Otherwise at the present rate of encroachment in another ten years there will be nowhere on the North York Moors where some unnatural object is not in view. One of the last strongholds of wildness and adventure will have been lost and the Lyke Wake Walk will be no more.

Note: In recent years the Moors Search and Rescue teams have been needlessly called out on many occasions, simply because support parties have failed to contact walkers. Often walkers have been safe at the other end when police and rescue teams have been looking for them at great expense. On occasions they have withdrawn from a walk and have been safely sleeping in a nearby farm whilst the search went on. It is absolutely essential that anyone who retires from a walk, or who has missed a support party, should ring the police or get some passing motorist to ring the police at the very first opportunity to let them know he is safe whether he knows he has been reported missing or not. And support parties should not panic. In reasonable weather conditions there is not really much danger to anyone on the Lyke Wake Walk. Do not call the police until you are sure something is wrong. Try to have an agreed contact telephone number for messages — and use it if a rendezvous is missed. On the other hand there have been one or two classic cases of rescue when people have fallen and twisted an ankle and there has not been a strong enough party to get them to safety without help.

Additional Note [January 1979]: The numbers now doing the walk mean that the main consideration for all concerned must be to avoid disturbance to others. *Parties must not stop in Osmotherley or Ravenscar at all between 11.0 p.m. and 7.0 a.m.* Anyone reported as doing so will be disqualified. Go straight to the Reservoir/Sheepwash car park and start from there. Official signing-in books have been discontinued, but the Pollard Cafe at Ravenscar keeps a private one. A report to the Recording Angels at Potto Hill is sufficient (include S.A.E. and 10p per head for membership Card of Condolence).

In the Lyke Wake Country

HE who would enjoy the Lyke Wake Walk, and other such walks, to the full, must know the country intimately—its geography, its geology and its history. The North Yorkshire Moors, a National Park, are still comparatively little known and unspoiled, being away from large centres of population except Tees-side. Here are 600 square miles of wild moorlands and lovely valleys, many of them quite uninhabited. Nowhere else in England except the high Pennines could you walk for days together and never meet a soul. A lifetime is insufficient to know the whole area as it should be known. Here ancient superstitions are not forgotten, and an ancient language is still spoken.

From the long fertile Vale of Pickering rise first the Tabular Hills of Coralline Limestone, whose steep northern scarps, from Black Hambleton to Barns Cliff and Silpho, are always prominent in the Lyke Wake landscape to the south. "North of the Tabular escarpment", writes Dr. Elgee, "rolls a sea of heather-clad moor, one of the largest uncultivated tracts in England, the dominant feature of the district from time immemorial. Eight hundred years ago it was known as Blackamore. John of Hexham, writing in the days of Henry II, states that Rievaulx Abbey was situated 'in solitudine Blackaumor'. Leland speaks of the 'very brows of Blakmore'. Camden states that 'among the mountains of Blackamore there is nothing remarkable, beside some rambling brooks and rapid torrents, which take up all the vallies hereabouts'. Drayton's *Polyolbion* in 1622 mentioned 'large-spread' Blackimore'."

Geologically, the Tabular Hills are Middle Oolite and their conspicuous character is due to hard beds of Calcareous Grit and Coralline Oolite on top of 150 feet of Oxford Clay, itself above a band of Kelloway Rock. The high moors are Lower Oolite—Moor Grit and Fossilferous Grit on top of thick beds of yellow Estuarine Sandstones, separated from the underlying Lias by that very variable band, the Dogger. Though the main Cleveland iron seams are in the Lias, the Rosedale seams were in the Oolite—in the Dogger—and there also are occasional small pockets of coal and limestone.

The Lias beds are the foundation of our moors and give them much of their character — the steep northern scarp of the Cleveland Hills, and the deep narrow valleys, Liassic inliers in the Lower Oolite. At the top of the Lias, just below the ferruginous band of Dogger, occur the alum shales, a hundred feet thick. In the 16th century the Chaloners of Guisborough brought home to Cleveland the method of alum extraction. Aluminium sulphate was produced by calcination from the alum shale, dissolved in water, a potassium salt added, and the alum precipitated as a fine powder. New and cheaper processes killed this industry in the middle of the last century.

Below the alum shales is the Jet Rock, a series of shales sometimes so bituminous that they ignite spontaneously, as on Boulby Cliff. Hence the red colour of some shale tips. Jet itself is of uncertain occurrence, and though plenty of jet ornaments are on sale in Whitby they are mostly of Spanish jet. Yet in 1872 jet working employed 1,500 persons and the value of the trade was £88,000. There is a Jeater Houses between Thirsk and Osmotherley, and a *Jet Miners' Inn* at Great Broughton. "Striking a good seam" had a particular local application in Cleveland speech. Probably the last to be found and worked was by an aged jet miner in Rosedale, about 1885, near the Hamer road. Having no legal rights, he worked it at night, and succeeded in reaping the benefit of his experience and observation. Apart from iron, jet is the characteristic mineral of our moors. Nowhere else in England does it occur in such quantity or quality, and it has been known and used since Neolithic days. Prehistoric man, ancient Briton, Roman, Saxon, Dane, Viking and Norman have all admired and worn "Whitby" jet.

The high moors crossed on the Lyke Wake Walk are of enormous antiquity, having been a land surface since the close of the Chalk Period, three to six million years ago. Tropical plants grew on them in the early stages and the petrified trunk of a large cycad tree was exposed in a sandstone quarry below Scarth Wood Moor towards Sheepwash. There are one or two traces of Stone Age men just before or during lulls in the Great Ice Age, and the last survivors of these ancient hunters left pygmy-flints in moorland camps as at Cockheads, near Hamer, around 6000 B.C. "Like stray shafts of sunshine", writes Dr. Elgee, "their small imperishable flints illuminate the depths of gloomy avenues of time. They give us glimpses of skin-clad men spearing a salmon in the Esk, or stalking deer over the melancholy moors — of women tending campfires on the heathery knolls whence craftsmen in the intervals of flint-chipping swept an eye over their hunting-grounds rolling to distant land and sea horizons."

The stone-axe men of the Early Bronze Age who followed them on the limestone hills and elsewhere, and the long-barrow men still later (after 2000 B.C.), never inhabited the high moors, and I like to think the early hunters survived there. It was not until about 1000 B.C. that the mid-Bronze Age round-barrow people, who had come over from Denmark and the Rhinelands, began to inhabit the moors, driven to those inhospitable heights by other invaders from Central Europe, the Brigantes, a name probably meaning "Mountain men". About 400 B.C. from France came the Parisii who occupied the Wolds and drove the ancient urn people who remained there to join their relatives on the moors. When the Romans came to conquer the Brigantes and Parisii, descendants of the urn people were still clinging to the high moors behind long lines of trenches, living on in the primitive fashion of their ancestors. No one can say how long this lasted, but with the coming of the Anglo-Saxons the Britons in their turn had to flee to the moors, which likewise must have long remained a British island now in a Saxon era, as many Celtic place names bear witness.

There was a new series of Scandinavian invasions, with the Danes in the ninth century, and then the Norwegians. Some came direct, and there were some from Ireland, through Cumberland, bringing with them some Gaelic-Scandinavian place names. Farndale may be one. Barnscliffe, the cleft through which the waters of Bloody Beck, Jugger Howe Beck and Derwent find their way, is the Gaelic *bearna*, a cleft between two hills. It is probable that Norwegians re-populated parts of North Yorkshire after its harrying and devastation by William the Conqueror, and that immigrants were still coming in in the 12th century. Except for a few British names, the Scandinavian influence is paramount in our place names as in our dialect. The few Britons who remained on the high moors, whence the last of the aboriginals must by now have long since vanished, were probably not exterminated but just swamped by the Norwegians, who were attracted to the moors and the dales perhaps because of the resemblance to their native land.

The Romans left the high moors untouched save for Wade's Causeway. The Britons left a few names and some traces of Celtic fields near Commondale, Wardle Rigg, and Cloughton (south of Ravenscar). But the Bronze Age Round-barrow People or Urn Folk have left their monuments all over the moors. Their barrows or howes (O.N. *haugr*, a mound), and their standing stones, are our landmarks from one end of the Lyke Wake Walk to the other, though most have been given Norse names by later invaders. These people buried some of their dead unburned—the ordinary folk, perhaps—but the chiefs and leading members of the tribe were all cremated before burial, and the remains placed in urns under the barrows. Dr. Elgee thought there might be 10,000 barrows of various sizes on the uplands of north-east Yorkshire. The idea of cremation was probably to prevent the ghosts of the dead from returning to trouble the living, and some of this superstition lingered on in the dales until modern times in the throwing of charcoal into graves. It is perhaps echoed in the Lyke Wake Dirge—"Fire an' fleet an' cannle leet".

Sometimes these burials are also marked by stone circles like the one on the ridge between Bilsdale and Tripsdale, the Bridestones. Other stone circles and standing stones are connected with cere-monial—perhaps sacrificial—rites, with sun-worhsip and worship of a mother-goddess (derisively named the Old Wife in later folk-lore). Whether always associated with fertility rites or not, many of the standing stones must have been useful then, as they are to us now, as landmarks and guide-posts, for no doubt the sea-roke often came down on Botton Head and Shunner Howe as it does today! Many of the howes and stones lie in long lines, as on the ridge south from Carlton Bank, and on between Ryedale and Bilsdale, or right across Fylingdales from the Bridestones above Grosmont to the barrow groups on Maw Rigg above Langdale. Still more remarkable, however, are certain well-marked settlement sites on Danby Rigg, Crown End above Baysdale, and in many other places where whole cemeteries of barrows, entrenchments, hollow cattle-tracks, hut-sites and the remains of small fields have been traced. One of these is at the beginning of the Lyke Wake Walk, near Scarth Nick, and one at the end, between Pye Rigg Howe and Peak.

Some of the urn folk's sites are those of farms inhabited to this day. They themselves had sheep and cattle and primitive agriculture. Their pathways ran mostly along the ridges, north and south, but there is little doubt that they would use the high water-shed for east-west crossing, and that we tread often in their footsteps. "Their ultimate fate", says Elgee, "is shrouded in darkness. Somewhere, at some time, a woman's deft fingers moulded the last urn, the wind drifted the smoke of the last funeral pyre over the moors, and the last cairn was piled over the dead." We who walk the high moors now cannot but be conscious everywhere of these long-vanished people.

The Lyke Wake Walk,
Mile by Mile

LYKE Wake Walk may, of course, be started from either end, but I prefer to walk towards the sea. The Beacon Hill triangulation pillar is 400 ft. higher than the bar of the *Raven Hall Hotel* — and a bar is a better place to finish at than a bleak moor top! Moreover, the prevailing wind is from the south-west (in the days when we stooked corn at Goulton Grange we pointed our stooks to Scarth Nick!) and the heather tends to lie towards the east. Try to battle the other way against a strong west wind and you will see what I mean.

There could be no finer starting point to a grand walk than this highest point of Scarth Wood Moor, close to the medieval signalling point of Beacon Scar and the television booster station. It may be reached from Osmotherley, up the road to the booster station (this is a public footpath, but unauthorised cars are not allowed to use it); from Ingleby Arncliffe (with its excellent *Blue Bell Inn*) by a steep climb from Arncliffe Hall, past crags where the eagles nested who gave this place its name, and which now provide one or two good rock-climbs; from Mount Grace Priory (the only considerable remains of a Carthusian monastery in England), by a track up through Arncliffe wood which is now re-planted by the Forestry Commission; or from Swainby via Scarth Nick, which means travers-ing that part of the route twice. Cars can conveniently be left in the car park at Scarth Nick or in the park near the reservoir, from where a much shorter track goes up to the start.

From this steep scarp you look right out over the Cleveland Plain, northwards across the Tees into Durham; while west-north-west in upper Teesdale you may see Durham's highest mountain, Mickle Fell, 2,591 ft., 43 miles away. A little to the south is the narrow gap of Swaledale, with Nine Standards Rigg perhaps just visible beyond. More nearly west across the great Vale of Mowbray is Wensleydale, with the flat top and steep northern scarp of Pen Hill (1,685 ft.) 28 miles away. South-west, beyond Northallerton, you may even see Buckden Pike (2,302 ft.) and Great Whernside (2,310 ft.), about 34 miles away.

On all these you must turn your back and look east. If the right wind does not for once prevail you may well remember the old weather saying, "T' wind i' t' east's good for nowther man nor beast". It is 35 miles as the crow flies, to the bar of the *Raven Hall Hotel*, but, as one casualty remarked, "It wasn't crows that measured these miles, it was b— —vultures!" As you will walk there are 40 miles of heather and bog between you and the sea. You will cross three main roads, and walk a mile of secondary road, but even so you may never meet a soul in all that distance, and apart from a cottage in Scugdale now, and Wheeldale Youth Hostel later, you will pass no human habitation.

Facing you first is the front line of Cleveland Hills, half of them concealed by the rugged bulk of Carlton Bank. But just peeping up far beyond you may see Botton Head, 1,489 ft., on Urra Moor, ten miles on in the journey you are about to start. You may, of course, choose to go slightly south of east, over Near Moor, or up Crabdale Beck, to the Shooting Box, over Whorlton Moor to Cock Howe, down Trinit ridge into Chop Gate, and so up to Botton Head by Bilsdale Hall and Medd Crag. This is a magnificent crossing — being more or less that described so breezily by A.J. Brown in *Tramping in Yorkshire* [*North and East*], *Part Eight — Chequers to Chop Gate*, but it involves much deep heather — and there is plenty of this to follow. The "classic" route by the Cleveland Hills is the one to choose, with its incomparable views over the Cleveland Plain, a patchwork quilt of rich grass and arable fields far below, stretching away to industrial Tees-side or bounded on the east by Roseberry Topping, 1,052 ft. (Odinsberg of the Vikings) and Captain Cook's monument on Easby Moor, 1,064 ft.

If each peak is taken direct, there will be just over 2,000 ft. of climbing and slightly more downhill running to Hagg's Gate on Clay Bank top (842 ft.). This forms a distinct first section (three hours taken fairly fast) different from the rest of the walk and the finest of introductions to it. What does make a first-class training walk is to do the round tour via Cock Howe and Bilsdale Hall to Botton Head and back by the front line route. I would recommend everyone to do this before attempting the Lyke Wake Walk itself. The 20 miles of tough and varied going are equivalent to half the Lyke Wake Walk.

But here we are still at our starting point — waiting perhaps for 12 noon as our zero hour. Immediately in front of us is Scarth Wood Moor, sloping away down to Scarth Nick in front, and tilted southwards towards the Sheep-wash in Crabdale Beck and the new reservoir, below which the beck has become Cod Beck and remains so until it joins the Swale near Topcliffe. ("Cod" probably Welsh "Coed" — Wood).

One of the farms where the reservoir is was called Wild Goose Nest. I doubt if a wild goose ever nested here, but gus is a Celtic word for wood, and so is coed as in Bettws-y-Coed—where else could "Cod Beck come from? In certain lights, of storm, or evening sun, the reservoir adds much to the beauty of the hills. At other times it seels all too artificial and it will be many years before it becomes really part of its wild surroundings.

Scarth Wood Moor itself is full of interest. Presented to the National Trust in 1935 by Major G.H. Peake (grandfather of the present Lord Ingleby, of Snilesworth Hall), it contains a number of Bronze Age barrows, and some ancient walling, but its main interest is geological. There are three faults, one along the line of Scarth Nick itself; in fact the whole moor between the Survey Pillar and the Nick has slipped vertically down in two sections, 100-115 ft. Then, in the Ice Age, the great glacier which came down from Scotland and the Cheviots, 1,000 ft. thick, dammed up a lake in Scugdale. The overflow eroded the 50-yard wide trench of Holy Well Gill on Whorlton Moor, while a smaller lake near Coploaf eroded a similar valley below you now, running from near Sheath's cottage (ruins) to the sheepwash—when the ice melted back to a line from Coploaf (Old English *cop*, the top of a hill, and *loaf*, a lump) to Live Moor, the level of Scugdale Lake dropped; those two channels were put out of action, and the torrent poured through to gouge out the deep channel of Scarth Nick (from Old Norse *skarthi*, a notch or cleft—also the nickname for a hare-lipped man, and still a good North Yorkshire surname).

You make for Scarth Nick first, along the wall, through the gate and across the open moor. Do not be tempted to take the left-hand track, which is the more obvious one, especially in the dark. It leads into bracken. You must now be well to the right of the wall, looking all the time carefully ahead to pick up the line across Scugdale to Live Moor. The road through Scarth Nick is the old drovers' road across Black Hambleton and was certainly a road long before the Romans came. When the plains were mostly forest and marsh this was the main route from York and Malton to the crossing of the Tees at Yarm, and it was commonly used until the railway era.

Cross the road just above the cattle grid, and you will see a finger post *Ravenscar 39 miles*. This, with the black discs marked LWW, have been very kindly put up by Lord Ingleby along what was previously rather a difficult route to find across Scugdale. Follow the black discs over Coalmire towards a knoll of grey shale practically in line with a hedge and wall going straight up the nose of Live Moor beyond. The wall is your next objective. To reach it go down the shale slope to the "Limekiln Road" which goes left to the game-keeper's cottage at Shepherd's Hill.

Jink slightly left across this green lane and down a hedge when you will strike the footpath running from Shepherd's Hill to Harfa Bank. This is now well indicated. It keeps well above a duck-pond, but soon afterwards you take a small wooden gate on the left, slanting across a

THE LOCATION

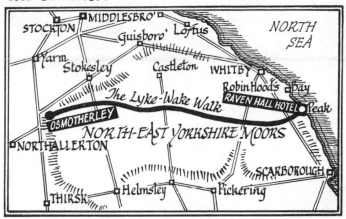

THE ROUTE : ━━━━

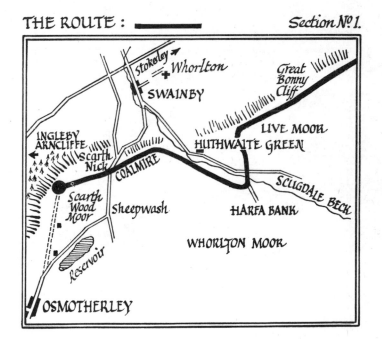

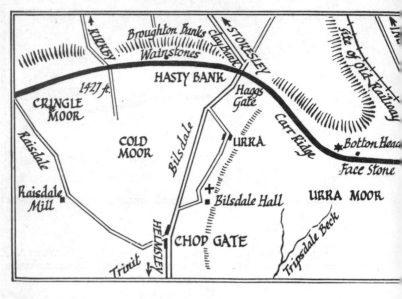

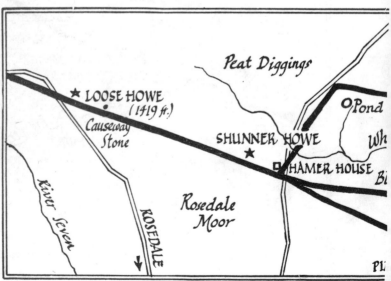

24

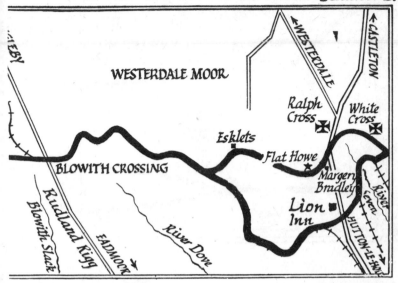

25

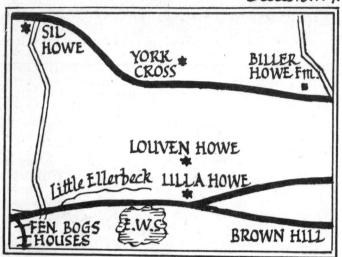

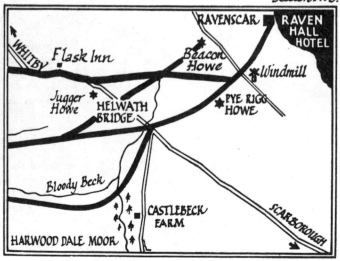

grass field to the ford below Hollin Hill. Please keep the gate shut. From here a metalled road goes up to Huthwaite or Heathwaite Green where there is a telephone box. Here a gate opens on to a track that leads past an old iron mine. Follow the black discs again and fork left at the second hedge towards some shale tips. Do not attempt to climb straight up.

Above the shale tips you will find the long wall and steep climb up "Knolls End" on to Live Moor. There is a black disc on a *Private Forestry* notice, and Lyke Wake Walkers have permission to use this sheep-drift. I have been told that the rather grassy moor beyond, Live Moor, used to provide common grazing for the donkeys which many Swainby villagers employed carrying coal and similar goods in the last century.

Some walkers, after struggling through Scugdale and up this steep knoll, have complained that "Live" Moor is scarcely an appropriate name. But from here all is plain sailing, along the main watershed, the boundary of the Ouse Catchment Board Area. All the springs and sikes to the right eventually flow to the Humber, those on the left to the Tees.

Looking north from Live Moor you see the prominent rounded outlier, Whorl Hill, beyond which lie the lands of Goulton Grange and Potto Hill, "Whorl" is from Old Norse *hvirfill*, a rounded hill top. Between Whorl Hill and Swainby lie old Whorlton church and the 11th century motte and bailey castle of Whorlton, stronghold of Nicholas de Meynell, a famous Lyke Wake walker in his time, poaching the King's deer anywhere between here and Pickering. East of Whorl Hill lies Faceby, an interesting example of a Scandinavian nickname becoming a place name. It means, in fact, "Fatty's farm".

Below Holey Moor, Little Bonny Cliff and Great Bonny Cliff are fenced in by the Forestry Commission, but beyond them you will see the line of shale tips along the 900 ft. contour which marks the old jet mines. Along the top of these goes an old jet miner's track which is sometimes useful when fog is thick on the tops themselves. It goes past John Quarry and Jackdaw Quarry to the old alum works on Carlton Bank. There is an inscription in Carlton churchyard to Tho. Sophle, Clarke to Capt. Christopr. Prissick's Allom Works, d. 1719. The route over the top of Carlton Bank is preferable, with long views back south down Thackdale (Snotterdale) into the upper part of Scugdale or over the long ridge between that dale and Raisdale to Green Howe and Cock Howe. Indeed at this point you are heading just slightly east of north, with the curve of the hills.

Go down the right-hand side of the alum workings to Carlton Bank top. Over the road is a grassy track leading up to Cringle Moor, locally "Cringie". At a junction of parish boundaries, about the 975 ft. level, may be found the Three Lords' Stone, the Lords at that time being Duncombe of Helmsley (now Feversham), Marwood of Busby Hall just below, and Aislesbury who at that time held

Scugdale. There is also an inscribed stone nearer the northern edge of the moor, which is the route you should take. Major Fairfax-Blakeborough noted: "On Easter Monday, 1905, a motor car driven by Mr Constantine ascended Carlton Bank to the amazement of everyone". Now "trial" motor cycles tear up and down the shale slopes shattering the peace of the moorlands above and the country-side below for miles. Much less objectionable is the quiet soaring, like great eagles, of the gliders that take off from Carlton Moor, though the Glider Club's wholesale levelling of the moor top is much to be regretted.

From Cringle there is a steep drop and a steep rise to Cold Moor (from which another fine ridge goes south to Chop Gate) followed by another drop and rise to Hasty Bank. You can if you wish bypass Cringle and Cold Moors by the jet miners' track along their northern face, but spurn the broad Forestry Commission track round Broughton Banks and strike up by the Wainstones (some fine short rock-climbs here) for the flat top of Hasty Bank. There is a good spring to the right—the Garfit side of the Wainstones. There are more rock-climbs further along the northern scarp of Hasty Bank, on Raven's Scar. Then you drop down to point 842 on Clay Bank Top ready for the first long spell and meal. This is a lovely spot, with the bluebell woods of Ingleby Bank on one side and Bilsdale stretching away on the other. The view north across re-planted woods is very fine, with the vale of Great Ayton and Kildale bounded on the far side by Easby Moor and Roseberry Topping. And if you think the smoky blur of Middlesbrough beyond a blot on the landscape, remember that there too is romance. A century and a half ago there were only two farms on a mudflat by the Tees where now is an industrial jungle of blast furnaces and steel mills—all built from the very heart of the moors whereon we walk.

From Hagg's Gate (where the old road went down into Bilsdale via Holme Farm) you now have to climb to the highest point of the North Yorkshire Moors, Botton Head on Urra Moor, 1,489 ft. (not given on O.S. map). Turn left along the stone wall that separates you from more Forestry Commission land. You are on an ancient paved causeway, a pack-horse track used much at one time by smugglers. The paving cannot be seen here but you will find it higher on the moor. The track goes through a narrow cleft in the cliff and through a small gate on to the open moor of Carr Ridge, going still along a wall, and with a line of boundary stones to the right. Further to the right is a long line of entrenchments along the western edge of Urra Moor. Though attributed locally to Cromwell, they are at least medieval.

To the north is the rounded valley of Ingleby Botton-*botton* being a Scandinavian word meaning just this type of valley; hence Botton Head. On Bartholomew's map this is referred to as Burton Head—and no doubt the surveyor thought he was being clever, since of course the local pronunciation of Burton would be Bo'tton. In fact he was quite wrong. A similar mistake occurs in Farndale, where "Horn End" has been substituted for what is really Hon End — *hon* meaning a nab. Below, in the Botton, you may see Midnight (house) and Siberia (ruins). A visiting Methodist preacher at Ingleby got a shock when told that the meeting next Sunday would be at Midnight. The navvies who built the Rosedale railway lived at Siberia. Near a boundary stone on the 1,300 ft. contour is Maiden Spring, the source of the Seph which flows down between Cowkill Well and the Cheshire Stone and so down Bilsdale to the Rye. If you can select any part of this walk above others this is perhaps the finest, but one of the trickiest in bad conditions. This great moor, burned badly by a disastrous fire before the war and only just recovering 40 years later, has the most deceiving contours. To the right two shallow dips join to form the wild rocky valley of Tripsdale, uninhabited and well worth exploring. The finest bilberries I have ever found grow there. At this stage you might approve the suggestion that the name is derived from O.E. *thripel*, an instrument of torture, whilst Urra probably comes from O.E. *horh*, filth.

Since the first edtion there have been many changes on Urra Moor. The guiding line across was once given by tufts of moor grass lying along the line of the old pack-horse track. There were also some boundary stones, some only a century old, some very ancient indeed. In the winter of 1960-61 Lyke Wake walkers reported that a bull-dozer was tearing out a fire-break right across the moor and had damaged surviving portions of the paved causeway which was the next landmark further on. Representations were immediately made to the Estate and to the N.R.C.C. In the autumn of 1961 a working party of Club members restored damaged portions of the paved causeway and excavated considerable lengths of it not previously known to exist. The fire-break remains and is now a broad highway over the moor, visible ahead soon after Carr Ridge is climbed, and with one branch going down to Bilsdale Hall. Unfortunately further Estate work on the fire-break in 1977-78 again damaged the causeway, little of which can now be seen.

Opposite the round barrow and survey pillar — "Round Hill" — which mark the summit, is the Hand Stone, the rough carving of a hand on each side, pointing *This is the way to Stoxla* and *This is the way to Kirbie and...*" The stone, like others elsewhere, probably dates from 1711 when the Justices sitting at Northallerton ordered that guide posts should be erected throughout the North Riding. A short way on is another stone, the Face Stone. This is certainly much older. It has a sinister Celtic-style face deeply cut on the east side.

In a 1642 Perambulation of the Helmsley Estate boundaries occurs this:

From Lambe Folde Stones goeinge N. to the Crosse with the Hande. (N.B. not the Hand Stone mentioned above). And soe forward to Bagerstone (the Badger Stone can be seen to the S. just below the source of Hodge Beck) leaueinge Cookinge (Cockayne) Rigg beeing the land of the Lord Duke of Buckingham on the East. And so goeinge N. wards vpp Barney Gill to the Streete Way. Then turninge N.W. to the bounder called Faceston.

Beyond a marshy piece where the fire-break curves round a little is another stone called the Red Stone or Rud Stone.

The present stone must have replaced a much older one. The name Red or Rud has several possible derivations. It is unlikely to mean red. It might be from Rood, a cross. It may be much older. **Redover** was an ancient name (Rievaulx Abbey Charters) for Hodge Beck which rises here—and this name probably comes from Welsh **rhed**, course, run, race; or **rhyd**, ford. Then the upright wooden stake in an old cow-house is called a rud-stake. And there is the Rudstone monolith in the E.R.

Near the Rud Stone occur the first surviving flags of the paved Causeway, which from the above quotation clearly existed as an old paved causeway—Streete—in 1642. The Rud Stone is in fact a cross **road** with the ancient tracks from Helmsley by Baxtons and Rowpa and from **Beadlam** Rigg (the perambulation route) mentioned in the Rievaulx Chartulary in 1145. The route from Beadlam was probably the Thurchilsti or Thorkil's Sty (**stee** is still good Cleveland dialect for a ladder or steep path) and this went on from the Rud Stone along what is now Turkey (Thorkil's) Nab.

The paved causeway is locally known as the sailors' or smugglers' trod. That it was used by smugglers is fairly certain, but it probably existed before smuggling became profitable. Packhorses were the main method of transport in medieval times. The track may have had older origins still—the Brigantes probably used pack-horses—but though the crossing must be an ancient one, lying as it does along a line of drier moor, with very wet and boggy moor only a hundred yards to the north, and springs coming out lower to the south, the age of the paving stones beyond the 16th century can only be conjecture.

Much of the paving must have been taken by Bilsdale farmers. Some flags from the surviving sections were built years ago into shooting butts. Otherwise the track can now be followed down to Bloworth Slack and beyond it (this was all new excavation) on the south of the railway to Bloworth Crossing. The probability is that it then went down Farndale where on some maps there is a place marked Long Causeway.

NOTE: Do not make the mistake of letting your support party (unless in Churchill tanks) go up or down Turkey Nab or Monket Bank (the track from Rudland Rigg into Farndale).

At Bloworth Crossing is another ancient road, going down Rudland Rigg to Kirkbymoorside, with branches into Bransdale and Farndale. Beyond this, as the line curves left, there is a sudden dramatic change. At one end of a cutting you are looking down Bransdale; at the other you have crossed the narrow ridge and are looking down into Farndale. Every dale is lovelier than the last. Another magnificent round tour to do, particularly in daffodil time, is to come over Botton Head, as you have just done, and leave the railway anywhere now, but the easiest descent is down Middle Head, into Farndale, and down the river Dove to Low Mill — six miles of daffodils — then back by the track across Bransdale and Tripsdale to William Beck Farm just below Chop Gate, returning to Broughton by Cold Moor Rigg. "Farndale" is possibly from Gaelic *Fearna*, alder.

The Rosedale Ironstone Railway is a fascinating bit of work. Iron Age man probably worked the Rosedale iron-ore, but in 1328 Edward III granted land for that purpose to the Rosedale Abbey nuns. Five hundred years later samples were turned down by Tyneside Ironmasters. They wrote that they were ashamed to see it lying on their quay! Then the story goes that Bolckow and Vaughan took a walk on the Cleveland Hills (the Lyke Wake Walk, no doubt!) and kicked a piece of ore. At any rate, with the Tees-side boom, Rosedale ore was found to be magnetic ore of excellent quality. Several thousand tons were carted to Pickering, then railed to Consett Ironworks, in Durham, for experiment. George Leeman, M.P., took the lease of Rosedale. He was Deputy Chairman of the N.E.R., and his associate Sheriff was Traffic Manager. In 1861 the Rosedale branch was opened. Five million tons of ore were taken out in the first 20 years, but less than half that was removed in the next forty. An article in the *Manchester Guardian*, November 9th, 1928, *Twenty Miles of Railway to be taken up*, remarked sadly that for the last few months trains had run only twice a week. The seams had worn thin, and there was depression in Middlesbrough, so that the line was to be demolished by T.W. Ward Ltd., of Sheffield. Incidentally, at the height of the boom, a rival company had projected building a line from Leeds right up Bilsdale, with a tunnel through Ingleby Bank, under Hagg's Gate!

After numerous bends, there is a long straight stretch of track over a mile long, with Esklets at the head of Westerdale on the left. "Gin Garth" on Westerdale Moor above Hob Hole is said to have been a storehouse for smugglers who crossed this way into Farndale, but the site was used for iron smelting and the "gin" was probably an engine.

And here at a pile of lime your fast three miles of cinder track (which can be very trying to the calves and ankles) come to an end. Turn left down to Esklets, which is an ancient farmstead once belonging to Rievaulx Abbey but is now empty and derelict. The track is marked by black discs again, and from Esklets turns back S. and S.E. a little as it slants up on to Flat Howe. Then up a line of shooting butts it turns due east again to come out at another ancient stone, Margery Bradley or "Old Margery", on the Castleton - Hutton-le-Hole road half a mile south of Ralph Cross.

Ralph Cross was always a place of succour — money used to be left on top for needy travellers. One of these accidentally knocked the cross over a year or two ago, and soon after it was repaired a gale blew it over again. A threepenny bit has now been brazed on top — but it would be better not to climb it to see. A flask of hot coffee, if you are lucky enough to have a support party, would be very welcome at Old Margery. Mechanised supporters can then go round the top of Rosedale, down to the Abbey, and back up what is now a good motorable road to Hamer, your next stop. Meanwhile, a mile of metalled road takes you past Fat Betty, a most charming white cross set in the heather. This forms part of a line of white boundary stones which, if you wish to avoid the next two miles of road, you can happily follow. Indeed when they cross the road a second time just past the Fryup Head by-lane, and bend towards Loose Howe (1,419 ft.) they are your guide for three good miles across a great stretch of moor and bog to Shunner Howe.

The track marked on the map over South Flat Howe, or the old line up the boundary stones between Flat Howe and South Flat Howe is also much used, although previously objected to by the estate.

An alternative to all this is to go along the railway for about two miles past the Esklets track until soon after crossing Blakey Gill a short and easy path leads you left direct to the *Lion Inn* at Blakey. From Blakey, drop down to the line again round the head of Rosedale till opposite Loose Howe; from the first wall and grass fields on the right it is an easy climb up to the boundary stones again. This alternative is strongly recommended during opening hours, and it also avoids three miles of hard road. Brian Jones at the *Lion Inn* welcomes Lyke Wake Walkers, camping is available. There is an old cockpit at Blakey (the name means Black) and coal pits near by. Two hundred years ago the inn was a marketing centre for corn from the dales and fish from the coast.

Just past Loose Howe you will cross another ancient flagged causeway and a stone marked *Causeway Stone*, 1864. This is another of the tracks used by smugglers from the coast coming up through Great Fryup Dale and down into Rosedale. The marsh in the hollow below needs careful negotiating. From Loose Howe you may catch your first glimpse of the three radomes of Fylingdales E.W.S. beyond Shunner Howe.

Half your journey is now over and here some Lyke Wake wag raised a cairn and cross with the following inscription:

> *Poor old chap, he did try hard;*
> *He died to get his Dirger's card;*
> *Here he lies now, just half way;*
> *And here he'll stay for many a day.*

(The cairn, like him, has since sunk into the bog.)

As you draw near to Shunner Howe (another fine Norse name) there is one small pine tree to the left. There are more in the slacks that go down into Bluewath Beck, and in that part of the moor are vast peat deposits controlled by the Danby Court Leet, where farms in Glaisdale have rights of turbary. We had the grazing at Glaisdale Head Farm in 1955 and it was while cutting peat here one lovely August day, with the heather purple all around, that the idea of the Lyke Wake Walk occurred to me. Unfortunately all this area was burned in 1976. By the time you have come down from Shunner Howe and Hamer you will actually have covered 23 miles with 17 still to go. If you make straight for the ruins you will have to wade through deep heather. Keep to the track by the boundary stones, which is, incidentally, the Cleveland boundary all this way, and the going will be easy on to the road. Hamer is a good point for a support party to meet you, but camping is not permitted.

The old inn is a sad ruin now, its fields gone back to moor. The last occupant, George Boddy, died there in 1936, but there are still members of the family lower down at Hartoft who run their sheep up here. Indeed, one member of the family, now a schoolteacher, has done the walk. In the old days this was a very flourishing inn in summer, and often a saver of lives in winter, though there are stories of some who didn't reach it, but perished in the snow in Wintergill or by Bluewath Beck. One old man travelled around selling corks. His bleached bones, identified by the scattered corks, were found near an ancient sheepfold when sheep were washed in the hot days of summer. Joseph Ford, who was born at Hamer in 1870 and died at Castleton in 1944, tells this story in his *Reminiscences*, for his mother was a good customer of the old man. One night two young men, Atkinson and Eddon, died mysteriously in one of the rooms, overpowered it was supposed by fumes from newly-plastered walls. They are buried at Rosedale Abbey.

Until about 1870 there was often heavy traffic past Hamer, for this was one of the main roads from the south up to Egton and Whitby; hence the names of London Ho. and York Ho., farms in Glaisdale. In addition, the Hamer coalpits (marked now by mounds of shale behind the inn) were in full swing. Farmers from Glaisdale and Eskdale took wagon-loads of coal to Cropton and Hutton-le-Hole, bringing loads of lime back for their fields. It was poor quality coal, and in a thin seam — about 1 ft. 8 in. You can still find plenty lying around, and it burns all right! It was drawn to the surface in curfs (strong boxes) by a horse-wheel. As many as 20 wagon teams might be drawn up at Hamer then. A famous man who must have frequently called here was Captain Scoresby, the navigator, who lived at Cropton, and who drew many of his crew from there for whaling expeditions from Whitby — men who quarried lime in winter and hunted whales in summer; who carried great whalebones back with them to Cropton, and who once fought off the Press Gang in

Whitby harbour, and probably celebrated their triumph here at Hamer.

And now ahead of you is the crux of the whole walk. Coming over Shunner Howe you would be able to see much of your route ahead — Simon Howe beyond the great sweep of Wheeldale Moor, and just to the left of Simon Howe, but far beyond, Lilla Howe, which marks the final stretch to Ravenscar. To the south of these lie the tabular hills in an imposing phalanx, Broxa and Blakey, Levisham, and Leaf Howe with its thin rectangle of trees.

It is the moor ahead, Wheeldale, which can break your heart and lame your legs. There is a good track now by Blue Man i' t' Moss, but avoid Wheeldale Gill (afforested). Or from Hamer go south-east to the intake wall corner, then, turning more easterly, you will see two rooks (piles) of stones more or less in line. Keep to this line until you see the High Pinkney shooting box, which must be kept a few hundred yards to your right. (It provides good shelter in case of need.) Take care that you have not gone too far south to the other shooting box on Middleton Moor. You should now strike a staked track which goes almost northerly for a short way then veers east along the long nose of Wheeldale Moor until it reaches the Stape Road. Go straight across this and down to the Roman road — "Wade's Causeway", or the "Old Wife's Trod" — a first century link between Cawthorn Camps and the coast near Whitby. A Y.H.A. sign indicates the track down to the delightful stepping stones across Wheeldale Beck below the Lodge, a pleasant place for a short halt whether by sunlight or moonlight.

Coming down from Wheeldale Moor you will already have picked your line almost straight from the stepping stones up Howl Moor on to Simon Howe. The place names hereabouts are full of historic interest, particularly Wardle Rigg, to the south. In the Yorkshire Inquisition of 1252 it is "Waldel" Rigg — the Rigg above the dale of the Welshmen, *wal* being from *wealh*, the Anglo-Saxon term for the Britons, This suggests, therefore, that a colony of ancient Britons was still inhabiting this wild part in Anglo-Saxon times, and as late as when the parish boundaries were laid down, since the Blue Man is in all probability the British/Welsh *plu*, parish, and *maen*, stone, or parish boundary stone, as it still is. You will also find hereabouts Brown Howe and, further on the route, Brown Hill. There are other Brown Hills, elsewhere on the moors, often tipped with barrows; *Bron* is Welsh for a breast. Compare Brown Willy in Cornwall and the Pap of Glencoe.

Beyond Simon Howe down the left-hand side of Crag Stone Rigg there is easy downhill going on springy moss to Fen Bogs Houses on the Newtondale railway. There is a very easy crossing here to Ellerbeck, but if you strike this line anywhere else you may have great difficulty crossing the bogs, particularly at Fen House. Both Fen Bogs and Fen House are deserted ruins now. (This area is now a Nature Reserve.)

The preserved Whitby-Pickering railway line was one of the earliest — and most beautiful — in the country, having been opened as a horse railway in May, 1836, with the great George Stephenson himself as consulting engineer. The length of 24 miles cost £4,000 per mile, and there were nine bridges of "Baltic Wood" over the Esk. Round Newtondale Well a mid-summer Fair was held. The Scar was also celebrated for hawks. In 1612 a Crown Commission into the privileges and extent of the Lordship of the Royal Manor of Goathland reported that "There hath been hawkes bred in Newton Dale on Killingnoble Scar, which the inhabitants of Goathland were charged to watch for the King's use".

Fylingdales Moor was in military occupation for many years, and there are undoubtedly some unexploded missiles still lying about even though the moor has been cleared. Hitherto no walkers have met with any accident, but in October 1958, some soldiers who were clearing the southern part of the moor met with a fatal one. Every walker must judge for himself therefore, and I can take no responsibility for any accidents. In daylight, with care, Fylingdales should be safe — but it is at your own risk. Avoid all unusual objects (none reported since 1970).

The direct route lies to the right of Little Ellerbeck stream, and walkers must be careful not to follow the main stream round to the south. Lilla Howe is the smaller of the two Howes you now see ahead, and is once again surmounted by Lilla Cross, reputed to be the oldest Christian monument on these moors, recalling an act of heroism in the 7th century.

The Cross had been moved to Sil Howe for safety during Army occupation and was returned to its proper home by Dirger Graham Leach, Whitby R.D.C. Engineer, in the summer of 1962. From Lilla Howe strike due east well to the right of Burn Howe Duck Pond. Make east for Burn Howe, and do not be tempted by the slope to Blea Hill and the sight of trees and fields beyond — a view which in misty conditions is so irresistible as to make the most experienced moorman think for a moment that his compass is wrong! Equally, do not be attracted by the slopes into Derwent basin on the right. Cross the ravine of Jugger Howe beck at the corner where the beck turns east, and on the other side you can follow an army road. There is then just a short bit of moor and marsh to the Whitby-Scarborough road at Helwath Bridge (hella O.N., flat stone, wath a ford).

For a long time we thought that the Early Warning Station being built on Fylingdales would completely block the Classic route. Fortunately its boundary fence is south of Little Ellerbeck, though that section of land is retained by the Air Ministry. The Classic route may be adhered to, and on an easterly crossing the Warning Station buildings do not obtrude as much as we feared, though the spoliation of this wild and lovely moor is a matter for profound regret. There is now a good track up Little Ellerbeck or the hard road outside the

E.W.S. northern fence may be used.

For anyone who wishes to avoid this monstrosity altogether there is an alternative "northern" route which is very pleasant and quite safe but goes through more inhabited country. It is the most northerly allowable and parties straying into Egton Bridge and Grosmont are disqualified. From Hamer you turn N.E. up the Egton Bridge road for almost two miles. Past some new afforestation on the left, a cart track goes off to the right eastwards to the Pike Hill Moss peat diggings. South of this track is a large pond which might be welcome on a warm crossing. From the tumulus and standing stones on Pike Hill make due east for Three Howes, a lovely crossing on short heather. Passing south of Randy Mere reservoir where the pine trees seem always heavy with scent, you go on through Thackside Farm down to Beck Hole, a lovely little village which again seems always full of the scent of wood smoke. The beer at the *Birch Hall Inn* is excellent, and thus fortified you can face the long climb up past Hawthorn Hill to Sil Howe.

Sil Howe and its quarries are on that remarkable line of volcanic eruption known as the Whinstone Ridge, which stretches right across by Lonsdale and Great Ayton to the Tees. This is now the line you take. You may indeed follow the right of way by Foster Howes, Ann's Cross and Louven Howe and Brown Hill. Brown Hill lies between the river Derwent and Bloody Beck (it was Bludebec in 1268). You might follow this all the way down to Lownorth Camp and find a path through Harwood Dale Forest and over Staintondale Moor to Ravenscar, but a better route is to cut off to the left at the tumulus (627 ft.) on Pike Rigg—beyond Brown Hill—and strike a path going down into the Jugger Howe ravine just below the Bloody Beck junction. From here you can go up through the wood by Helwath Beck to the bridge or cut over on to the road above Castlebeck Farm.

A still shorter and pleasanter way is to turn east by York Cross (a fine stone set in a plinth two hundred yards off the main track). Follow the heather-drift and aim for the next main outcrop of the Whinstone Ridge on Pike Hill. Keep on, aiming to the left of the shoulder of Blea Hill and keeping John Bond's Sheephouse—a few dressed stones left down in May Beck—and Cock Lake Well on your left. There is indeed a little well here if you have time to find it, but no lake. This area is now planted, but the Forestry Commission have left a footpath across for Lyke Wake Walkers.

From Blea Hill you keep due east along Biller Howe Nook Slack to Billera Cottage, Brown Rigg and the *Flask*, with another drink well earned. From the *Flask*, after about a mile of main road, you can turn off (just after an embankment) over Stony Marl Moor, with the radio pylon on Beacon Howe as your guide. Or you can keep on again to Helwath Bridge, and rejoin the Classic route.

Between Helwath Bridge and the Harwood Dale signpost a narrow footpath curves off east through the bracken and heather, joining in about half a mile a proper forest road. If you miss this track you may flounder about in heather, bog and bracken for half an hour. The forest road leads straight over Pye Rigg Howe and over a short bit of moor to a lane past a windmill, a good landmark. Then you can let yourself go down the last mile of metalled road to the *Raven Hall Hotel,* and may the bar be open!

*N.B.: This route is now little used. From Jagger Howe most people take the army road and cross Stony Marl Moor to the Beacon. The Beacon is now accepted as a finish in order to keep people out of Ravenscar village.

History of this Moorland Way

THE Lyke Wake Walk has been done from the earliest times. An Eolithic (or pre-Palaeolithic) huntsman did it from west to east, but went off route a bit, dropping a flint implement at Eston Nab. He was caught on Wheeldale Moor by the Great Ice Age, and by the time he got through to Whitby and dropped another he had become Middle Palaeolithic! This must be the longest recorded crossing. Bronze Age Man crossed frequently on feud or foray, or merely with a funeral procession, singing an early form of the Lyke Wake Dirge. In Roman times part of the Ninth Legion from York made an attempt, and none of them was ever seen again. Two Territorial officers, however, Justinianus and Vindicianus, managed to get through and actually signed the book at Ravenscar in the form of a stone inscription. They built the first club hut on the site of the *Raven Hall Hotel*. This was inadvertently burned down by a Scandinavian party that crossed in the opposite direction some years later and having got into difficulties early on, named two of the obstacles Helwath and Bloody Beck. Caedmon and other Whitby Abbey monks are thought to have done the walk, but when William the Conqueror tried it he got hopelessly lost on Bilsdale West Moor.

One of the best walks of which we have record was by Edward II in 1323, on his way to visit Nicholas de Meynell, the Chief Dirger of the time, at Whorlton Castle. He came from Lockton by way of Hamer and Danby but didn't really qualify for membership of the Club as he took a whole week. A good "Wake" was held at Whorlton however, and "Alice the Red-haired and Alice de Whorlton" sang *Simon de Montfort* and "got 4 shillings for their pains". George Villiers, second Duke of Buckingham, made several attempts at the Walk without success and was finally in 1687 evacuated as a casualty from Urra Moor to Kirkbymoorside, where he died calling for a pint of ale. A worthy Lyke Waker of his day was John Andrews, M.F.H. of the Roxby Hounds, who kept the *Ship Inn* at Saltburn, and was one of the leading smugglers of the 18th century. He usually crossed on business with a pack-horse train of bootleg brandy. Whenever a smuggled cargo was landed, the message that "Andrews' cow has calved" was flashed across the moors. Unfortunately this message was used once too often and it is recorded that one Thomas Stevenson of Marske hunted the Roxby Hounds "while Andrews, M.F.H., was in gaol".

Coming to more recent times Dr. Frank Elgee, that great archaeologist and naturalist, whose writings I have quoted freely, foresaw the modern Lyke Wake Walk. Mentioning the front line of Cleveland Hills Dr. Elgee writes:

The watershed between the basins of the Tees and the Rye lies on the very edge of this noble range of hills. East of Urra Moor the watershed divides the drainage of the Esk and the Derwent, and steadily declines to 800 ft. on the moors south of Robin Hood's Bay. The width of the moors from West to East, from Osmotherley to Peak [Ravenscar] is not less than 32 miles.

As a boy in Middlesbrough I knew Dr. Elgee, curator of the Dorman Memorial Museum. He was examiner for the Scout Naturalist's Badge, and lent me 6 in. maps to look for medieval flagged causeways. I wish I had been old enough to know him better. His work breathes a passionate love for the moors where he spent his life. No one who walks the moors should fail to read his *Early Man in North East Yorkshire*, published in 1930. He declared: *My love(for this region) has been a powerful motive in the creation of this work. Otherwise I question whether I should have been able to summon up enough patience, endurance, or courage to study so much arid archaeological literature, or to examine dusty antiquities in so many museums. But amidst the bracken and the ling and with the companionship of wind, sun and rain, archaeology became a pure joy and the life of the past a real presence.* There speaks a great man, whose name has been carved by his friends on a block of stone near Ralph Cross.

When in August 1955, I put forward the idea of a 24-hour walk across this route, David Laughton and other members of the York Mountaineering Club quickly took up the challenge. I really had no intention of doing the whole walk myself, but got so wrapped up in studying maps and working out the best route that I just had to do it. Brigadier Willans of Fylingdales P.T.A., and I, hurled map references at each other amicably over the telephone for a week and finally he wrote reassuringly that "Mortars will be firing to the north of the range but I will ensure that no rounds fall south of Stony Leas—500 yards north of Lilla Cross". At the starting point on October 1st, the Y.M.C. ten members and I were joined by two Middlesbrough Senior Scouts, and by a Guisborough Forestry Commission engineer who finished the walk all right but whom no one has seen since! Mr. T. L. Goulton presented the "Goulton Tankard" to the new club. My farm, Goulton Grange, had been with his family as far back as the 12th century. Doubtless some of the Goultons or Gautons were companions of that great poacher and Lyke Waker, Nicholas de Meynell.

One of the three Y.M.C. girls who started, Joyce Allen, dropped out at Goathland with bad blisters, but was so determined to do the walk that she tried it again four weeks later in much worse conditions, accompanied by John Poulter and Malcolm Walker. They did it east to west this time, reaching the pillar in a heart-rending finish with only half a minute to spare. Joyce later married John. She could hardly do less.

By this time the walk was attracting a lot of attention. The *Daily Mail* had linked the first crossing with an Everest and Kanchenjunga party in Wales. The headlines were "Celebration — seven climb 500 ft. cliff" — "Exertion — 12 walk 34 miles". At the Yorkshire Mountaineering Club dinner on November 19th, 1955, I commented on the sense of comradeship developed by the joint effort of the Walk and suggested that this be carried forward into a Yorkshire Himalayan Expedition of our own. Three of the six members who went out to Kulu, Lahoul and the Parbati in 1957 were Club members.

Meanwhile the next outstanding crossing was accomplished by a party of members of North Riding Youth Clubs, in May 1956. Jim Tierney, of Grangetown, reached Ravenscar with five minutes to spare. Two years before he was in an orthopaedic hospital encased in a spinal jacket. Members of Whitby Round Table had a breakfast of bacon and eggs for the walkers at Hamer.

In June, Eric Hopkins and Derek Wilson, of the York M.C., did a very good crossing in 13½ hours. "My room at Osmotherley was most encouraging", wrote Derek. "It overlooked the graveyard." Chris Readman, a Middlesbrough Rover Scout, did a lone crossing the same weekend in about the same time, and the race was now on for a 12-hour crossing. The Yorkshire Ramblers Club descended on Osmotherley in force on Saturday, 15th June, and on the 16th, 20 men set off from the triangulation point about 4.30 a.m. P.A. Warsop took just a minute under the 12 hours, and three others were under 13 hours. The President, H.L. Stembridge, wrote that he would not like to see such a grand walk become a race for the fastest time. The important thing was for a Club to be able to get a good proportion of its active members across from dawn to dusk. Some of the Ramblers felt the walk was not *quite* so hard as their Seven Peaks walk.

My own view is that part of the fascination of the walk is in being on some of the route at night, and I am not at all sure that the qualification for membership of the Lyke Wake Club should not be to do the walk in 24 hours — and not in less than 20! "Speed" attempts were shortly after this settled by Arthur Puckrin, a Middlesbrough Queen's Scout and later Police Cadet. He first did the walk in August 1956, in 21 hours, sleeping for five hours at Glaisdale Head. "The going was extremely wet and tough." Shortly afterwards he did it again, leaving the triangulation point at 6.47 a.m. and reaching Ravenscar at 5.27 p.m. — 10 hours 40 minutes. The following Friday he set off at midnight from the pillar, reaching Ravenscar at 10.10 a.m., breaking his own record by 30 minutes, and *set off back again,* arriving at the pillar at 11.19 p.m., *both ways* in just under 24 hours. There was 1-inch of snow at Hamer on the outward journey.

Among the Yorkshire Ramblers was Crosby Fox, who led their own Expedition to Nepal in 1957. While I was high in the snows of the Parbati I heard the terrible news that he had been swept away with two Sherpas by an avalanche, and that he lies now for ever in the Himalayan ice. David Pearson, a Foundation member, died in a Cairngorms climbing accident, Easter, 1959. After a serious accident in 1962, H. Ivers asked for a lost Condolence Card to be replaced, "I do hope I may have one because unfortunately I shall never again have the opportunity to do the walk, or in fact any other walk".

No one crossed between July 1956 and April 1957, except Arthur Puckrin—three times. Then some Scarborough boys went over. Richard Featherstone wrote:

> We started in heavy mist but with the rising of the sun and wind this cleared and we received some glorious views of fold on fold of moor with shafts of sunlight through the mist. We clambered about on the Wainstones. We saw many bootmarks. Some marks of commando sole variety, were in both directions. We imagine they belong to that admirable type who is reputed to have done the walk both ways in under 24 hours. He must have more than commando soles.

In October four members of the Selby Round Table crossed with great *éclat*. None of them had done any walking before, and one of them did it in gum boots! Having lost the way on Fylingdales, they staggered on to the Scarborough road and were accosted by a policeman. "Now gentlemen", he asked politely, "what are we up to?" "We're doing the Lyke Wake Walk", they said. "The *what?*" "Er — we've walked over from Osmotherley." "Oh", said the policeman, "a great friend of mine is the constable there — give him my regards when you get back". Croaking that they had no intention of going back, ever, the gallant four struggled on to the very sea shore by Stoupe Beck, only to find that they had overshot the mark and were now faced with a 600-foot climb back up the steep cliff to the *Raven Hall Hotel*. When at last they crawled to the top — bitterest blow of all, the bar had closed! They had taken 20 hours but "please bear in mind that we are a Talking Club, not a Walking Club, hence the reason for making such a task of it". The weekend after, David Laughton, Stella Boaden and Ann Pendegrass, Foundation Members, did an east-west crossing with John Elliot, also of the Y.M.C., in 23 hours with no support party, carrying all gear, and one with Asian 'flu. They then walked down into Osmotherley and hitch-hiked home to York, having been on the go, apart from an hour or two in the Wheeldale Shooting Box, for 40 hours.

There was no further crossing till May, 1958, when Rowntree Moor and Fell Club went over. R.K. Thompson (who was over 50) did it in just over 11 hours. In July three York Senior Scouts got too far north on to Egton High Moor, and Sneaton High Moor, covering 47 miles and having only two minutes to spare. But a fortnight before them Hull C.H.A. had done one of the toughest of all crossings — the party including one girl, Jean Penrose. Frank Harrison wrote:

> Up to Loose Howe the going was extremely wet and there had been some mist. From Loose Howe (reached at 11 p.m.) we were never able to see more than five yards ahead even with the aid of torches and every few steps we would be up to the knees, occasionally deeper, in very wet bog. It was impossible to follow the boundary stones to Hamer and we had to march on a compass bearing. This was rather tricky without being able to fix on anything and was not made any easier by continually falling down. I consider we did well to make the Hamer road just north of Egton fork (**Author's note**—they must have come right through Glaisdale Danby peat diggings near Cockheads!). Unfortunately we assumed we were south of what was to be our camp at Hamer, and walked for a good three miles in the wrong direction. Eventually we arrived in camp at 3.30 a.m. Three of the party, including myself, seized up here but the remaining nine set off into the mist at 6 a.m. At Fen House they had to wade waist deep to cross the marsh and a further two gave up at the start of the Salt Road. The seven who finished walked over 50 miles in just under 23 hours. We are all eagerly awaiting the next supper. (Jean Penrose was made a Mistress of Misery for this achievement.)

Meanwhile the Territorial Army had arrived on the scene, two officers of H.Q. 150 Infantry Brigade getting across in May. It was they who decided the miles had been measured by vultures rather than crows! They were followed by the 5th Battn. the West Yorkshire Regt. 1 Northern Command Royal Signals T.A., headed by Lieut. Col. J. Kilner and Major David Willett, and including Capt. M.E. Clarke and three other members of the W.R.A.C./T.A. crossed successfully in 19 hours. This party was the first to get the Lyke Wake Walk on the television screen. On the last stretch over Fylingdales the Major gallantly gave the order to advance, "It's boggy in front, but we'll go *straight through*. It doesn't matter now". Whereupon he disappeared up to his waist in the coldest and smelliest bog of the day. It was a Sergeant in this party who made the classic remark, when told that it looked as though the bar would be closed when they arrived, that what he was afraid of was that the b — — cemeteries would be closed.

The last across in 1958 were Mrs Cowley and myself, with Harry Tilly (another Himalayan climber) and Mrs Tilly as support party. At the time of the first walk Mrs Cowley could only act as support party. Our daughter was born four weeks later and promptly christened Heather. Since then my wife has done most of the sections but this was the first time she had been able to leave three children long enough to do the walk (she has crossed twice since).

The following June we provided support for Mr and Mrs Tilly. Sunday, June 14th, 1959, is a day none of us is likely to forget. There was bright uninterrupted sunshine from 5 a.m. to 9 p.m.

We had camped in Wheeldale and the walk was over by 9 a.m. Ravenscar was a glory of blue sea and golden broom. At least 60 other walkers were out including 34 members of Territorial Army Medical Units from Leicester, Birmingham, Derby and Leeds. Thirteen of these, including Col. G.A.W. Neill, M.O.H., Barnsley, and one Nursing Sister, got across. Some of the party finished comfortably in the inn at Rosedale and others less comfortably in the police station at Whitby! I was invited to join those who did succeed in a champagne celebration in the *Raven Hall Hotel,* after which some of us went swimming in the pool there.

The Pudsey Rambling Club did a crossing, followed by a Middlesbrough Boys' Brigade and other Youth Clubs. Whitby Round Table were again at Hamer dispensing refreshment to anyone who looked like a Lyke Wake Walker—that is to say, with a haggard and hungry expression and a distant look in the eyes.

The first crossing reported in 1959 had been in May by Alan Crouch (who immediately afterwards sailed for a two-year post as meteorologist in Antarctica) and Martin Roulson (Halifax). That also had been a hot day. They strayed into the bracken of Wheeldale Gill and had to sit in the beck for half an hour to recover and cool down. Alan even went to sleep in the beck! They then went too far south into the Newtondale ravine near Pipel Head, and waded up the stream from there all the way to Saltersgate. York Hoboes made the first of their crossings. Other names to appear now were H. Gillies and N. Addison, of Stockton C.H.A., who have done the walk many times since and in some very fast times. Chris Readman, who had done a 13-hour crossing as a Rover Scout in 1956, now crossed in full army kit, with rifle, accompanied by another infantryman from the D.L.I. Lt. Richardson followed their example. But the outstanding Army achievement of this year was undoubtedly Col. Neill's. He crossed three times in three months, with various units. When he suggested that the Club should have an appropriate tie (black, with silver coffins) we immediately appointed him Sorrowful Shroud Supplier, a post which seemed eminently suitable for a distinguished M.O.H.

In 1960 the avalanche started. S/L. Gikffins had a Royal Navy representative with him. They surveyed the route first in a helicopter. All three Puckrin brothers—Arthur, Richard and Philip —signed the book so frequently that I had to ask for a consolidated annual report from the family.

Two Scarborough Y.M.C.A. boys, R. Morris and M. Bayes were obviously not keen on writing so sent a detailed map instead. Two other boys wrote, "We are not Scouts or anything—just schoolboys". Many schools now began to do the walk, particularly after the G.C.E. examinations. Middlesbrough High School, Pocklington, Red Barns, Redcar, Coatham Grammar, York Technical and the Durham Colleges were prominent. Grangefield Grammar in particular became a familiar name. First across from there was T.A. Whittingham with some 1st Fairfield Scouts. R. Clubley and P. Bell soon became veterans of a dozen crossings.

Another enthusiastic group were boys from Castle Howard School who have passed on their enthusiasm to other approved schools such as Dobroyd Castle, Todmorden, and among them they have done many crossings.

E. and M. Thompson, father and son (47 and 19) of Sheffield, crossed in 18 hours. The son, a diabetic, had had daily injections of insulin for the past ten years. Barnes and Peacock, of Darlington, did it at their fourth attempt. G. Dawson, a "gas engineer", returned 14 hours 10 minutes. Huddersfield Rucksack Club and York Rovers and Rangers made successful attempts. Peter Long and Wendy Harvey did the first of their crossings. They are one of our engaged couples whose special steadfastness of purpose I cannot but admire. (They are now married but still do the walk; their daughter Susan — my god-daughter — did a first crossing in September 1977 aged 12).

The Karabiner Club party knew they ought to be singing the Dirge whilst they did the walk, but they did not know the words. They improvised with the following:

'Twas brillig and the Dirgers three
Did mesh and werble in the vast;
All mimsy was the croaky knee
And the moan gasps outpassed.

Beware the Lyke Wake Walk my son!
The miles that grind, the heather hell!
Beware the glugsuck bog, and shun
The frumjious unexploded shell!

Now while up Urra Moor they sped,
The morning sun with face aflame,
Came wiffling over Danby Head
And frizzled as it came!

One, Two! One, Two! And through and through
The vorpel toes went snicker-snack;
And Farndale Head and Wheeldale Gill
Were soon galumphing back.

On December 7th, I did a third crossing myself, setting off to walk E.W. at 8 a.m. This was the first winter crossing — winter by weather if not actually by the calendar.

I took the northern route and Stony Marl Moor was crisp and white with frost. A pale sun peeped through the mist into the little valley below Biller Howe, and the keen air carried the scent of gale, that aromatic little bog plant that is still used by some to brew gale beer. By York Cross the hoar frost was so thick that I seemed to be walking through acres of white heather—and I was wet to the knees as it melted. Beck Hole was full of the scent of wood-smoke, and beer was like iced nectar. I dried myself over the **Birch Hall** fire for an hour. On the wooded slopes beyond, the frost lay thick as snow. The afternoon grew dark on Pike Hill. Grouse shot cackling from the heather with a scattering of frost particles. I hurried to get through the bog to Loose Howe before darkness and just succeeded—but then cut too far north into some peat diggings. The main road was like glass.
I sat over the fire in the **Lion** for two hours and got dried again, leaving at 8.30 p.m. There were heavy showers of sleet, and the main danger through-

44

out was slipping on icy pools. I went flat on my back twice, and broke my compass, but I was on home ground and didn't need it now. The half-moon filtered through and I have never had an easier or pleasanter crossing of Urra Moor. Frost and moon between them showed up the narrow track. I little thought that a month later the bulldozers would come in to ruin that track for ever.

I had to crawl up the steep part of Hasty Bank on hands and knees, so icy was the slope. From the top the view was fantastic. A vast ocean of grey mist lay over the plain, billowing up against the rock precipices of Raven's Scar and between the pinnacles of Wainstones. The tops were clear, but once I dropped below I was enveloped in cold clammy fog. I did not greatly enjoy the last two hours—finish at 2.30, home at 3 a.m.

Records had ceased to stand for long in the Lyke Wake Club. At the Wake on the 10th Tony Whittingham announced his intention of leading a party across on the shortest day—or longest night—December 21st/22nd, which he did, with Richard Clubley and Peter Bell.

Winter had now ceased to be a close season. I.S. Sutherland opened 1961 with a January crossing. On February 12th Tony Whittingham and Peter Bell went across for the third time and a new name appeared—C.C. Bosanquet (14). B. Richards and D. Clubley dropped out after Fylingdales.

This could have been due to the dash through deep heather as darkness descended, or to the shock of stepping over a notice upon which was boldly written in red paint the word "**MINES**".

This was Campbell Bosanquet's first crossing. From now on I received an average of one report a month from him, crossing with one or other of this group of youthful experts—nine in one year.

It now becomes impossible to mention a tithe of the crossings reported, or quote from more than a few of even the outstanding reports. The Lyke Wake Walk seems also to inspire everyone who does it to a peak of literary achievement, like those who "approached Simon Howe looking like Old Testament prophets arriving at Mount Tabor".

On a May crossing P.L. Tweddle reported a layer of snow on the moor. It hailstoned at Wheeldale Lodge and rained on Fylingdales.

Castle Howard reported that their pedometer registered 66 miles when the walk was over—a measure of the energy used, perhaps, if not the distance!

On April 1st, J.S. Pallister:

Waited at the start till midnight, enjoying the beautiful panorama of lights from Tees-side, and Whorl Hill rising dimly from the plain like an island from the sea. By 5.30 p.m. we sheltered beneath the bridge at Moorgates. Rain was becoming heavier and visibility began to diminish. My friend (Paul Wiles) now looked in very bad shape and was slowing up all the time. He admitted his heel was causing him pain, and though he was still keen to finish I realised that with the riskiest part to come he ought not to continue, for he could not finish in his condition (he got a lift).

I now forged on on my own. The skyline had vanished in darkness and I could not take a bearing, but checked my compass every five minutes to make sure I was going due east. (He was a few hundred yards too far north, and struck terrible trouble in the succession of ravines near Wragby.) I slithered in total darkness down a steep slope to the beck and crossed it. Trees in a wood here had been cut down and I blundered into them. I was now soaked through and there was as much swamp in my boots as out. I resolved to go on in spite of all obstacles. Twice more I had to cross streams in deep gullies. Then I saw headlights—hit the road—reached Helwath with heavy sleet falling—and so to a good meal at the **Pollard Cafe.** My friend hitched to Whitby where he saw a doctor. He was suffering from a strained Achilles' Tendon.

Miles Frankel wrote from London begging me to say for his parents' benefit that there was no danger on the walk. His party started from Boggle Hole on April 19th:

We finished standing almost knee-deep in mud in the middle of Glaisdale Moor when our 24 hours were up . . . The next day three of our party had to return to London sharing 16 blisters between them. And so there were two of us left. We set off again from **Pollard Cafe** on 21st and this time our navigation was more correct.

And this time they got right across with just 15 minutes to spare. M. Williamson's party ran into a "bull-type cow" near the *Flask* and a soggy type bog on Wheeldale Moor.

By this time we were all tired so finding one dry spot decided to stop till daylight. We simply put the cape groundsheets down and tried to sleep on them. It was very cold and wet. At Chop Gate it was no use packing at this stage so we pulled ourselves together and staggered up the murderous climb out of Bilsdale. After hours of torture we reached Scarth Nick, and the last drag up to the pillar. It now started to rain hard but sitting with our backs to the pillar and our capes over us we were alright.

Giggleswick, St. Wulfram's, Nunthorpe Grammar, Langbarugh, Victoria Street, Wellesley Nautical and Newham Grange Secondary Modern joined the schools section; Cleveland Technical and Loughborough the colleges. Somebody did it in dinner jacket, top hat, umbrella and brief case — and swore the equipment was ideal. Several parties of Middlesbrough boys went over and with one of them in August went Mrs. M.L. Hunt (52), in just over 20 hours of slow but determined walking.

A beautiful sunrise—pelting rain—saw my friends a mile ahead—arrived very tired into Wheeldale—the young men very kindly waited for me—Ravenscar 2 a.m. a lovely starlit sky but a cold wind—I do hope I am now a witch. P.S. My husband says I have been a witch a long time.

When Stockton Co-op. Youth Club did the Walk, the three girls decided — at 4 a.m. on Fylingdales — that they would feel better if they had a good cry. They did!

The first all-women's party went over in September unsupported.

It consisted of Marilyn Wardman, Rowena Jones, Joyce Hodgson and
Pauline Bastow.

> On Urra we were tempted—but not **too** much—to follow Venus. The stars were
> wonderful . . . After a sleep in the heather on Loose Howe we rubbed sleep
> from our eyes and followed the boundary stones to a superb gold and pink
> dawn. Met two men doing the walk in the opposite direction . . . Bloody Beck is
> well named, isn't it?

Pamela Bastow of the Cleveland Rambling Club has led many
parties across. D. Lewis did the Walk the first time in both directions
in one week. The Cleveland Mountaineering Club also does an
annual crossing usually led by Alf Rout. I was with them in June,
1961 (E. — W.) in lovely weather till the last ten miles when wintry
rain lashed us. It was Rita Cox's first crossing but she won a mad race
over the last hundred yards of heather to the survey pillar. By
contrast Mike Williamson on his fourth crossing reported having to
crawl the last few yards! Morale had not been improved on Cringle
Moor by seeing "two fit-looking chaps running in the opposite
direction. These we later discovered were Arthur and Richard
Puckrin making a record-breaking crossing". Indeed they were.
After Harry Gillies had done 11 hours 8 minutes in May for the full
Classic route on June 10th Eric Derwin flashed past other members of
the C.M.C. (including me) to finish in 8 hours 38 minutes (by Cock
Howe).

These two crossings aroused some controversy about respective
routes and records. There was much discussion about having a
correctly supervised and timed race confined to the half dozen
members who had already done under 12 hours. Arthur Puckrin,
however, was recovering from an injured knee. I was very solicitous
that we should make sure he was better before we fixed a date. On
July 10th he wrote:

> I am glad to say that my knee seems to be alright now. I tested it yesterday,
> Sunday, over the Classic route and managed to complete the course in 6 hours
> 39 minutes 26 seconds. My brother Richard was with me but dropped back near
> the end and only managed 7 hours 16 minutes 26 seconds. Times—Start
> 7.38 a.m., Clay Bank 9-12, Ralph's Cross 10-26, Hamer 11-5, Ellerbeck 12-31,
> Ravenscar 2-17. We passed about 20 people who were doing the walk whilst we
> were on the way. I noticed with regret that a path has been trodden for much of
> the way, though this allows faster times. I should be alright for an October
> race.

I refused to accept seconds, and we settled on 6-40 — but Arthur
had effectively scotched the idea of a race, enthusiasm for which
vanished immediately! Instead, a television walk became the high-
light of the year. One Tuesday night *Tonight* programme rang up to
ask if anyone would be crossing the next weekend. I said that if not
we would lay a walk on for them, and sent a circular letter round to a
few of the experts. The vultures gathered immediately. Promptly at

the appointed time next night my telephone rang. By 10 p.m. I had 25 names from Hull, Huddersfield, York and Newcastle as well as the locals. In addition a fleet of support cars (with varied menus) was laid on. Arthur Puckrin was in the London-Brighton race for the Saturday, but said he would drive back overnight to join the walk!

Of course, as soon as we began planning, the television side of the walk, never more than a good excuse for a convivial crossing, began to seem rather a nuisance. When at the agreed 6 a.m. starting time the camera team hadn't arrived, I left Derwin, Gillies, Addison and the Puckrins behind at the pillar as models, and the rest of us started just half an hour behind schedule. We reached Clay Bank in 2½ hours.

The cracks caught us up on the railway. Arthur Puckrin, after coming 17th in the London-Brighton race, had driven back, crashed near Wetherby (not his fault), got a lift home in the very early hours, and came straight out to the start. Richard, with the whip-hand for once, and Eric Derwin, forged ahead right out of the cameras and no one saw them again till the finish (about 11 hours). Whittingham, Clubley, Bell, Gendle, Ken Smart and I kept together, did several sections three times for the benefit of the camera (that steep bank down to the stepping stones!) and finished in 13½ hours. I hadn't been so stiff since the first crossing!

Chris Brasher and the camera team joined us in the bar of the *Raven Hall Hotel,* and we gave a very powerful rendering of the Lyke Wake Dirge. But the pace had been too hot for several very experienced Dirgers. The saddest case was Frank Harrison, who dropped right behind from Ellerbeck; we found him at Helwath when we stopped the festivities to send out a search party. He'd been trying to summon up strength to crawl the last three miles (a knee having given way completely) but just couldn't. His one remark was that as he hadn't done a sixth crossing he wouldn't now feel he had to do a seventh!

Three weeks later I did another crossing with my wife, and we only saw land twice. I've always sworn I would never do the Lyke Wake Walk in really bad conditions, but somehow when everything is arranged and you get started it is very difficult to turn back. For this crossing we arranged with Peter Long that he and Wendy would take their car to Ravenscar, we would take ours up to the start, and we would then walk in opposite directions to each other's transport.

We started from the pillar at 4 a.m. with a clouded moon sinking and a light drizzle falling. The moon went, and pitch darkness caught us on Carlton Moor. I took a short cut—and missed the track! So with precipices around, and dawn almost due, we sat down in the wet heather for breakfast. Fifteen minutes later the utter blackness faded to dark grey. We were just two yards from the edge of the quarry, and five above the path. On any clear night there is enough light reflected from Tees-side to find the way along here, but in conditions of cloud and real darkness the cliffs on Carlton, and Cringle Moors, and on Hasty Bank, can be very dangerous.

On Urra we were right up in the cloud and drenched with wind-driven rain. Beyond Bloworth the railway embankments disappeared into a misty void—we walked on a narrow ribbon of land elevated above an ocean of mist. With the

The presentation of the Goulton Tankard outside the Raven Hall Hotel in October 1955, prompted the inauguration of the Lyke Wake Club.

The author on Cringle Moor.

March 2nd, 1963—during the first ski crossing.

E.N. Graham, R. Gibbon, and G.L. Tyldsley, pictured soaking their feet in Wheeldale Beck.

Midnight bivouac at Hamer by Hull C.H.A. (Photo: Fred Turner).

E.N. Graham, R. Gibbon, R. Pogson and G.L. Tyldsley are pictured as they prepare for a 2.45 a.m. start near the triangulation pillar on Scarth Wood Moor.

Dirgers and their support party at Old Margery.

Members of the Durham County Constabulary Cadet Training School at the start of their walk.

**Ralph Cross, on the central section of the Lyke Wake route.
(Photo: Jack Wetherby).**

Scarth Nick, looking towards Whorlton Hill. (Photo: G.W. Martin).

The signpost in Scarth Nick. The coffins and candles are part of the Lyke Wake Club's crest.

Jet Miners' Track on Cold Moor.

Whorlton Castle, former residence of the Baron Nicholas de Meynell.

Top left: The Face Stone on Urra Moor. Bottom left: Blue Man i't' Moss. Top right: The paved Causeway on Urra Moor known locally as "smugglers' trod". Middle right: The Hand Stone on Urra Moor. Bottom right: Fat Betty.

wind on our cheek as guide we hit the **Lion** exactly—and there were Harry and Diana Tilly with some dry clothes and a second breakfast (9.30). That strong south wind was the best possible guide and we consulted neither map nor compass. From the railway again there was a lift of cloud in Rosedale below— our first sight of land since we started! We struck the boundary stones in thick wet cloud again, crossed the road and floundered through the mud over Loose Howe. Knee-deep in the middle of the bog below, with rain pouring down, we saw two more drenched figures coming towards us—Richard and Philip Puckrin. "You're not doing the Lyke Wake Walk are you?" asked Richard. My reply is unprintable.

Further on we met two or three more, the sole survivors of some 60 scouts who had set off from Ravenscar in the early hours. Len Douglas and his wife were waiting on the Egton road and we ate lunch in the car whilst they got wet outside. As we moved off Peter and Wendy arrived, rather behind schedule. It now began to rain in earnest. On Pike Hill the heavens opened and I have seldom been wetter! But then as we came into Beck Hole the skies lightened once more and we actually saw green fields. The pace kept us warm—the only hope in bad conditions is to be fit and go fast—but we were glad of Len Douglas's hot tea and whisky at Sil Howe.

The rain gradually stopped, we got to the **Flask** before dark and to Ravenscar at 7.0 p.m.—15 hours.

Driven mad by the constant stream of Lyke Wake Walk stories coming into the *Evening Gazette* office, a team of reporters decided to do it themselves. Four of the five succeeded—and got good press coverage!

In spite of bitter winds and snow, there were many crossings in the winter of 1961 62. Some Physical Education students from Loughborough wrote for information as they wanted to do a thesis on the walk. I suggested they do it first, and they did—in January.

W. Greenwood set off from Scarth Nick on March 20th with 74 boys—some from colleges, some from various Approved Schools— "On looking back as I came to the cattle-grid it was a remarkable sight—the cortège stretched out back to the skyline." About half got across, but "this experiment with a large group proved many things, the prime one being never to do it again". P. Knowles crossed twice, from east to west. "When we arrived at Ravenscar at 9.45 a.m. we were told that we looked very fit. Then we explained that we had just come to *start!*"

Many will sympathise with W. D. Toulman who, alone and unsupported, did a first crossing, a navigational Odyssey, in April, 1962. Starting at 10.15 p.m., he went astray in Scugdale and did not reach Harfa Bank till 11.20.

How glad I was to find a black disc! So to the top of Live Moor—not very well named . . . On Urra Moor a mist blew up and I was lost again. Eventually I reached the northern edge of the moor which I followed east, more or less, till it curved off north. I then set off across the moor to where I hoped the railway track was. All went well till Wheeldale Moor. Navigating on this moor is a terrible problem, there being no landmarks. I met four girls, the first humans I had seen since leaving Osmotherley the day before. They said that the going was easier in Wheeldale Gill and I believed them.

After wasting much time on the side of the gill I regained Wheeldale Moor at about 1 p.m. Soon after a storm blew up and I had to press on expecting to end up as lightning conductor. I struck Newtondale much too far South and crossing the railway at 3.55 my spirits were at an all-time low. The Air Ministry constabulary were very obliging after seeing my letter signed by the Resident Engineer.

Bucked up enormously by the effect of this letter I set off to what I thought was Lilla Howe. In retrospect I do not think it was Lilla Howe as there followed afterwards a series of navigational blunders. On these moors, to me, one Howe looks like any other, as do the streams and moors. I reached a Howe, I didn't know which one, at 5.10 p.m. and afterwards crossed what must have been the embryo River Derwent. Soon after I found a track which I thought was the Army road on Jugger Howe Moor. It was not to be, for it was the track round Brown Hill. After wasting much time I decided to cut my losses and set off across the moor.

From now on it was a race against time and fatigue. I reached Helwath at 8.50 and by a bit of luck found the right track towards Ravenscar. I pressed on using a handkerchief soaked in water to splash my face in order to keep awake. I reached the bar two minutes before closing time, and seventeen minutes inside the 24 hours.

A very determined solo attempt against a lot of difficulties.

Later in April Miles Frankel crossed both ways in 48 hours, a considerable feat, especially as he came up from London to do it. On May 13th I led a party of farmers over—just to prove that in these days of mechanisation they hadn't completely lost the use of their legs. Derek Heath and George Heeley claimed never to have walked more than six miles before, and that after a golf ball, but they strolled over the full Classic route very nonchalantly in 16 hours. What really shook them was to realise, when they only had twelve miles left to go that this was as far as walking from home to Northallerton, something they would never dream of doing!

Also in this party was Graham Leach, Engineer and Surveyor to Whitby R.D.C.—the first man to do the walk on crutches! Owing to a damaged knee he had to limp the second half supported by a stout staff. Least, but not last of this party was John Cowley, 4ft. 9in., just a week or two after his fourteenth birthday. I think 13 is too early for anyone to do this walk, and had previously discouraged it. A fortnight later he insisted on doing it again in the reverse direction with his mother and me, despite heavy rain to Beck Hole and a bitter cold wind of gale force all the way.

Conditions had been very bad the week before too, when several parties crossed. Water was right over the top of the Wheeldale stepping stones. Gordon and Brenda Lewis did a second crossing though a year before they had written that they didn't expect they would ever walk forty miles in a day again. Mr. W. Brown, on his second crossing, also took his wife. They referred to the warped sense of humour of Lyke Wake Walkers, and suggested that anyone not satisfied by doing the walk once should be offered the services of a psychiatrist. Unfortunately our psychiatrist has done the walk twice himself!

A party of Head Wrightson draughtsmen held two training walks to show up any weaknesses and defects, and correct them before the actual attempt. "We realised on the first walk that it would be impossible to cure a lifetime of loose living in the short time at our disposal." A Stockton accountant, after a hard crossing, offered to send details of "a simple little device which acts as a cage holding off the bedclothes from what were my feet. Sleep is thus possible". British Titan Products, Reckitts' Computers and I.C.I. Engineering (Stress Analysis Section) joined the ranks of industrial Dirgers.

R. Clubley on his eighth crossing commented: "By now, one would have supposed that everyone realised that on this walk the shortest distance between two points is *not* a straight line."

Warren Kroeger, an American engineer from the Fylingdales project, complained of my calling it a "monstrosity", after all the trouble they had taken to paint the radomes duck-egg blue and plan the buildings to tone with the moors. He found it a beautiful sight as he first spotted it on the walk, while coming over Rosedale Moor. But he was proud to be taking the first L.W.W. tie back to the States. Arthur Puckrin did another double crossing, lowering his own record on the way there to 6 hours 19 minutes (16 hours 17 minutes both ways).

Alan Waller did several crossings, but one man he took over couldn't get out of his bath afterwards without assistance, and was off work for seven weeks. Alan also reported following a mouse along the old railway — in spite of every effort on his part to catch up the mouse drew ahead. Other mice, lizards and adders have been reported but this is the first to have made what seems a serious attempt at the walk. A peculiar double crossing was completed by H. Webb. Moving his car along from one point to another he did each section both ways in turn, in 48 hours. (Method repeated August 1978 by P. and E. Vaughan in 36 hours).

The most remarkable crossing of 1962 was done in September (at his second attempt) by Rev. A.E.C. Morgan, sometime Vicar of Holy Trinity, Wakefield. He had just passed his 81st birthday and was accompanied by his daughter Mari (17), by J. Cowley (14 — 4th crossing), C. Bosanquet (15 — 15th), and W. Cowley (46 — 16th). In spite of two bad falls Mr. Morgan completed the full Classic route in just under 18 hours in astonishingly good shape and became our very good friend and the Club's Cheerless Chaplain. Mr. Morgan boxed for Oxford as a heavyweight in his youth, and was keen on rugger and cricket. But however fit you are, 40 miles of rough moor is a longish step at 81. Most people would think it foolish to try. But for him it had been "a wonderful adventure". He went off next day for a week's fly-fishing up Teesdale.

At the other end of the age scale, one or two 12-year-olds got across. The last crossing of 1962 was by R. Clubley, C. Bosanquet, J. Cowley, J. Rattenbury and L. Stephens, on December 21st/22nd, making an attempt to complete the walk between sunset and sunrise on the longest night. In the conditions — their bootlaces were frozen stiff when I met them at Clay Bank — they failed by an hour to beat the sun, so took a rest and finished at leisure — though that's not what they called it.

Snow fell immediately after that and as it deepened in the early weeks of 1963 thoughts began to turn to the possibility at last of a ski crossing. Though there was good ski-ing on many Cleveland hillsides, first attempts at covering any distance were exhausting and disappointing. The snow was too soft, or had blown off the heather. It was not until the end of February that conditions became hopeful. Really heavy falls had weighed down the heather, melted and frozen. Another fall froze on top and finished the job. All roads were blocked and men had to be rescued from the Early Warning Station.

Every section of the walk was re-explored from the skier's point of view. With only twelve hours daylight, a new moon, and blocked roads we soon decided we could not safely and enjoyably complete a crossing in 24 hours. That would take expert skiers at the peak of fitness. After our week of exploration (in which some of us had already completed the whole walk once) we set off from Ravenscar Station at 1 p.m. on March 2nd—W. Cowley, J. Cowley, C. Bosanquet and D. Rich. Jugger Howe Ravine was the first exciting run—and stiff climb. Probably no one had been there, or on many other parts of the route, since the "Longest Night crossing" which two of the present party had been on.

Fylingdales was a vast Arctic tract, sloping down to the snowy Derwent basin. A hazy sun glared on the snowfields with a Himalayan effect. We saw grouse and fox-tracks, and in addition to our own previous ski-tracks, two new ones which perturbed us. (We found later they were made by J. Wastling and A. Mathieson, Wilton I.C.I., who had started from Ravenscar just before dawn and reached Bloworth at sunset. They finally gave up at Carlton Bank after struggling a long time in the darkness.) There was a long gentle run down from Lilla Cross (we could have stepped over the E.W.S. fence in several places) to Ellerbeck and on with a final swoop to Fen Bogs. Then as the sun set into Goathland for a night's rest at Church Farm.

On Sunday we climbed up to Two Howes again as the sun rose behind the three giant puff-balls of the E.W.S. It was a remarkable and I will admit quite beautiful sight in those conditions. A long slanting run down to the Stepping Stones, and Wheeldale Moor was excellent going in the crispness of the morning. Even the deepest heather was a level snowfield. So was the bog beyond Hamer, then from Loose Howe another long delightful run took us swooping down to the old line in Rosedale, which was like a Himalayan valley. Blakey at noon—and the road had been opened nearly to the inn that morning. The Bosanquet family had fought their way up with delicious stew to accompany the Lion's beer.

From there we skied in an ecstasy of snow and sun over South Flat Howe and down to the railway. We cut out some of its curves preferring to climb a little for the sake of the run down. At Bloworth two or three walkers struggling through deep snow eyed us enviously. We made down the fire-break to Chop Gate knowing the five steep climbs on the classic route would now be beyond our strength (though they had provided magnificent ski-ing on another day). The descent to Bilsdale Hall, where south-facing snow had melted then frozen, was exciting in the extreme. Apart from two or three short steep climbs the few hundred yards of main road from Seave Green was the only time we carried our skis. Unorthodox routes over drifted walls and hedges took us up on to Scugdale Moor. We went across the middle of Brian's Pond. Frozen solid and snow covered it was difficult to distinguish from the Arctic tundra all around. The sun was setting and the wind was bitter. Down through Snotterdale, a last tedious climb, and a hazardous run in the dark back to Swainby, and right to our own door-step at Potto Hill—7 p.m. 17 hours ski-ing, 30 hours altogether. On Monday the thaw set in—we had been only just in time.

It had been one of the pleasantest and most exciting weeks of my life. To know these moors intimately in every aspect for years then suddenly to find them transformed to this Arctic splendour, was an unforgettable experience. For months afterwards I thought of those wonderful snowfields, and could not face an ordinary crossing.

However, others came thick and fast. Several people, including K. Howells, and Peter and Wendy Long, did solo unsupported cross-ings. Mrs. M.L. Hunt (determined at 54 to attain her Doctorate of Dolefulness) was one of these. Mr. G.S. Jackson, C.B.E., Chief Constable of Newcastle, with Mr. H.H. Salisbury, Chief Constable, North Riding, and other distinguished Police Officers, did a crossing (and were accused of trespassing at Blakey!). R.W. Gibbs "followed a compass course from Blue Man. This course was obviously in error because we finished on Leaf Howe one mile south of the wrong shooting house". T.A. Whittingham (11th crossing) took an Imperial College of Science party which included Amir Murani of Uganda, who said it was "definitely tougher than Kilimanjaro". P. Bellamy became the fourth man to do a double crossing (35 hours). L. Tabner and B. Smith's support party were late at Ralph Cross and Hamer, lost at Ellerbeck, and couldn't light the primus at Helwath. P. Sherwood (4th) and R. Clubley (13th) sent in a report in the form of a Last Will and Testament, bequeathing seven pairs of worn-out feet to the Club Archives.

Some Newcastle doctors bivouacked en route in Black's Icelandic sleeping bags covered appropriately with polythene corpse-covers. A party from Scarborough "almost formed the filling of another tumulus". W.D. Toulman finished another crossing at the Mid-summer Wake after sleep-walking most of the way. On the same day a Northallerton G.S. party travelling east reported "somewhere in the bog we met a lone westward-bound figure with a huge pack and a fixed expression who lumbered past with scarcely a murmur in reply to our cheerful greeting. We later decided that he was not intentionally taciturn but rather at the speechless stage of exhaustion, as the last man in our file caught the words ' — —bloody walk three times and not finished yet — —.' " Alan Waller on a 7th (lone) crossing complained bitterly about this "solo" business which forced him to neglect a beautiful girl who was lacking companionship over Wheeldale Moor, and no one else in sight. A.G. Bell, Hull, reported that one of his party dropped out at Hasty Bank "explaining that he was under a misapprehension about the nature of the walk".

Newcastle dental students reported in the form of a three-act play. Sheffield General Hospital staff was led by B. Sellars, "a man of great pessimism". C. Booth and G. Hart met several other parties — "a member of one, dressed in a city suit, was in a state of collapse". B. Smith demonstrated superior fitness by doing handsprings across Fylingdales. D. Cook failed to clear Bloody Beck and recorded a depth of over 4 ft. "His feet had not touched bottom and the water had reached his chest when we hauled him out." L. Bulman "had no idea what the walk would be like — perhaps I imagined a bridal path right across, signposted all the way!" A. Puckrin took a family party over in 17¼ hours. The party included sister Eleanor (15), father

T.W. (65) and uncle H.A. (70). "I gave them the full treatment", said Arthur. A British Railways party boasted the motto "It's quicker to walk". Another party near the *Flask* "were actively discouraged by the occupants of a parked car. They knew the area well and made it quite clear that they would not in any circumstances risk crossing the Moor in the dark". The landlord of the *Falcon* discouraged another party by saying he had never dared set foot on the moor at all since a tractor disappeared in one of the bogs.

K. Olley described the walk as "a malignant meander over merciless moors". A. Waller reported (tenth crossing): "Going up out of Wheeldale we could have done with crampons; crossing Wheeldale Moor we needed snowshoes; coming down Urra Moor we were direly in need of Purple Heart pep pills; and nearer the finish we were so tired an ambulance would not have been out of place". Redcar Venturer Senior Scouts carried a coffin (polythene) across in April; one or two other parties had the same idea. R. Clubley's badge was seen at Liverpool University and he was appointed Chief Technical Adviser in a water speed race in coffins against a London college. An argument as to which way coffins should be propelled for maximum efficiency aroused the interest of the Professor of Fluid Mechanics and models were tested in a pressurised wind tunnel. The answer was, appropriately, feet first.

Another engaged couple, G.T. Robinson and Judith Raper, planned to make the walk the first stage of a complete crossing of England, Scarborough to Morecambe, a laudable ambition, but conditions were against them. They did 70 miles to well beyond Bedale with practically no sleep then had to give in. D. Mitchell reported: "A month ago my wife declared she wanted to become a witch, by the Classic route." They were accompanied by their 17-year-old son, and met an acquaintance "laying up iron rations (beer secreted in becks) for an attempt next week". Few people can imagine how dirty and disreputable a Lyke Wake walker can get. As these three approached the *Raven Hall Hotel* "three frightfully well-bred little brats with most expensive accents said 'What's this coming NOW? *They* won't be allowed in'!!" P.A. Sherwood picked a young crow up and carried it on to Live Moor. He intended to take it all the way—as the crow flies, so to speak. Unfortunately this one couldn't fly at all, so he left it. A B.O.C.M. party included four married couples.

A Cottingham dirger reported that one of his party "declined to go further at Hasty Bank, and retrospectively I think he was right". Margaret Green "may have inherited some of the Lyke Wake tradition from her grandfather, who was an undertaker". In August 1964 an undertaker actually did the walk, with John Dunning, farmer, and A. Lister, of Beverley. "The undertaker had not heard of the walk before but we managed to persuade him that he might be needed in a professional capacity, thus appealing to both his pride and his business instincts."

Sq.L.Carman, R.A.F., on an annual pilgrimage, commented "on the extraordinary number of boot soles along the route that have parted company with their owners". J. Bennington was so far gone at Simon Howe that he thought he heard an ice cream van playing chimes — the tune was *A Hard Day's Night*. Paul Sherwood did a 12th crossing by mistake — the mistake was to call in at a Potto Hill party on his way to the Isle of Man for a holiday. He found himself doing the crossing instead.

T.A. Easton crossed in one long thunderstorm, by the northern route, E.-W. He got lost in the murky streams beyond Beck Hole and at one point thought he was crossing the reservoir itself. He fell asleep by the firebreak at Botton Head and when he woke up set off in the wrong direction. He met one or two parties he had passed previously, and couldn't understand their surprised looks when he wished them luck against the dangers ahead. He did not realise his mistake till Bloworth Crossing. One girl passed him, her eyes tight shut and her arms held out in front of her like a sleep-walker. She was laughing hysterically. "To every group I passed I said in sorrowful tones 'It's worse further on'. It probably was, too, by the time they got there."

In July 1964 the Osmotherley Village Summer Games Committee asked the Club to organise a Lyke Wake Race in connection with the games. Profits from the games were to go to a fund for the new village hall. The Club does not approve of turning the walk into a race as a general rule, but this seemed a good excuse to give the speed-merchants a day out. Some complicated mathematics were involved in working out handicaps at various check-points. The Territorial Army provided support and medical assistance. A. Puckrin had the fastest time. 6½ hours.

This Race has become an annual event. In 1965 John Waind, a farmer, took 8½ hours to win the handicap on his second crossing. Ian Ashley Cooper, Paul Sherwood, John Cowley and a dozen others took under 12 hours. In 1966 Jeff Hall of Sheffield equalled A. Puckrin's race record of 6½ hours. Wendy Long has the fastest woman's time of 11½ hours. Philip Puckrin lowered the Race record to 5 hours in 1971 and in 1978 the first five (out of 55 finishers) were under 6 hours (Ken Robinson 5.21). Brenda Yule lowered the women's record to 7.30 with Audrey Collinson close behind (7.54) and Pauline Calder (8.33). Mary Atkinson, the "Galloping grandmother," did 11.46 and beat her own husband!

Arthur Puckrin lowered his record time (not in the race) to 6 hours 13 minutes. Some disturbance was caused in Lyke Wake and athletic circles by a runner (with a strong following wind) claiming a time of 4½ hours. There was no prior notification of this attempt. In October, members of various Harriers' Clubs ran a race of their own and Mick McDonald set up a new official record time of 6 hours 1 minute (by Classic route to *Raven Hall Hotel*]. In the 1968 race,

Philip Puckrin set a new record of 5 hours 15 minutes. Double crossings (both ways in 48 hours) have been completed by J. Ashley Cooper, J.M. Cowley, P.A. Sherwood, J. Adams, A. Waller, D.M. Cowley and just one girl so far, Jane Saunders. (A. Anholm, J. Tait, D. Dale and B. Price are among several who completed doubles in 1968. J. Gray and L.Kulscar did a quadruple in 78 hours in June.)

Arthur Puckrin also completed three consecutive crossings in 32 hours 15 minutes, for the 120 miles. Start 4 a.m.; Ravenscar 10.18 a.m.; back at start 6.58 p.m.; slept Hamer 11.45 p.m. to 4.30 a.m.; finished Ravenscar 2.15 p.m. He admitted to having sore feet after this. Arthur has progressed through various editions of this book, from Queen's Scout through police cadet and police constable to law student. He is now a barrister.

During 1965 Hull was very prominent. Crossings were made by Hull City Police, Hull University and Hull Steel Radiators Ltd. Ted Emberton saw a party heading across Wheeldale Moor in quite the wrong direction — straight for a bog he had fallen into himself on an early crossing. Nobly he chased after them, to be greeted with the remark that they knew what they were doing and had no intention of landing in Wheeldale Gill. "If only they knew where they were going to land", said Ted, "but I daresay they found out sooner or later." Doncaster Expedition Club were put on the train by Peter and Wendy Long, after a hard crossing, and did not wake up until the train reached Retford.

K.L. Doggett wrote from York: "On Good Friday our amateur woodwind quartet descended on Osmotherley. Our flautist was providing transport, but the oboe, clarinet and bassoon were walking. The fog was so thick we had difficulty finding the way even on the firebreak, and on the railway I stepped off an embankment and fell 15 feet. The bassoon fell flat on his face in a bog. We tried to find a drier path but got lost and trudged through bogs worse than those we were trying to avoid. The real test came that evening when we had to go out and play chamber music. We kept dozing off in the odd bar's rest."

Charlie Thomson of Leeds led a party of six and the youngest of them was 50. Charlie is 53, 6ft. 3ins., 18 stone, and promised a donation to Club funds if any member was taller, older, and heavier than him! At 5 a.m. on a cold May morning J.R. Carter passed a man asleep in a deck chair on Blakey Ridge. Another party in July passed several bodies at the same place laid out in polythene bags. A French girl, Mlle Savoye, wrote that she had "enjoyed the walk in spite of blisters, because it gave confidence and I found out what my possibilities were". Michael Bellamy of Redcar found soaking in bog water for 24 hours to be an infallible method of getting rid of corns.

D. Brown crossed with a friend who "saddened, saturated and saturnine, remembered a previous appointment and departed from Blakey in a northerly direction". Brown then contrived by skilled compass work to travel through heather and bog all the way to Wheeldale Lodge "parallel with and at 50 yards distance from all well-marked paths, if any". J.S. Cooper admired the voluptuous curves of the railway track. He fell over before starting the walk and nearly hamstrung himself on the port side. This however balanced a weak starboard Achilles tendon, and he progressed through the heather with the action of a pregnant chorus girl. On Holey Moor he met a weasel doing the walk in the opposite direction.

C. Brownlee of British Titan Products met a lizard on Fylingdales and was envious of its ability to propel itself forward. Near Jugger Howe ravine he found a cycle cape — it was rotten and crawling with earwigs, but inside was a can of Ind Coope's Long Life beer! Victor Scott "got the idea after reading your book in which you make everything sound so nice". One of his companions was told by his doctor to stay off work for a week afterwards, his blisters were so bad. Katherine Clough of Northallerton with six other girls did the second recorded crossing by an all-female party, a third (first east-west) was done by Judith Brownridge and three other York witches.

Brian Lowther took ten hours in the race. "A lot of people were staggering round Osmotherley afterwards, whether from the effect of the race, over-indulgence in alcohol, or just being stunned by the price of the dance, I do not know." T.A. Mulqueen's party had intended leaving the Trig point at 3 a.m. but they weren't able to find it. "It doesn't make for confidence if you get lost before you've found out where you are." G.C. Kilvington got lost several times but wrote "The Lyke Wake Walk is made for a little suffering, a little pride, and, I hope, for all who tread its glorious ways, a great appreciation of its beauty and untamed wildness".

Group Capt. Wright, C.O. Fylingdales R.A.F., and Mrs Wright did the walk in June. It was a clear sunny morning and they felt a sense of foreboding when they realised they had to walk three times as far as the eye could see. Barbara Wright nearly gave up at Wheeldale "but the thought of having to go through the whole agony again drove us on". Julia Ferguson composed a ballad as her report:

My muscles are aching, my feet give me pain,
But give me a week and I'll do it again.

R. Williams commented at Hamer that the crossing was a good half done. W. Blackett replied that he felt a good half done himself. York Rowing Club got across in October, and another crossing was led by Mr E.B. Harrison Raw, Hair Stylist to Ladies and Gentlemen.

The year 1966 began with a crossing on New Year's Day, in somewhat inebriated condition and undoubtedly record time, by Dirgers George Heeley and Derek Heath. They flew over in 18 minutes. Garside and Robinson crossed in appalling conditions on January 26th. The Wheeldale stepping-stones were under water and they were swept off them by the spate. They managed to scramble out, wrung out their socks(!), and arrived at Hamer in heavy mist. The railway cuttings were full of snow.

In February, Brown and Tunnicliffe met a different hazard. At the E.W.S. they were apprehended by a poetic R.A.F. policeman who wanted an audience for his poems. In April, P. Belshaw reported "yet another lapse into masochism — the third in 18 days. My toes have now turned a funeral purple under the nails, like ripe damsons in the fall, and soon I fear they will drop off". M. Nellis of Scarborough had a girl in his party who sat down in the middle of Wheeldale Moor and insisted on having a taxi to take her home.

Mary Feverhelm, "a 38-year-old mother", of Scarborough, composed a·poem whilst in a mustard bath after completing the walk. On his fourth crossing in May with his wife, P. Belshaw "came across an extraordinarily moving scene. Round the starting pillars were the bodies of some half dozen successful moonlight dirgers, slumped in complete abandon, like baggage awaiting collection. Out of respect we spoke in whispers and tiptoed away. We left this Henry Moore group with the sun shining in a flawless sky, and a spectacular mist inundating the valley below like a petrified Arctic Sea".

Interesting crossings were also reported by a Home Office Course in Child Care, by the Elmsall School of Motoring and by three Artificial Inseminators from the Cattle Breeding Centre at York! Alan Hoffman heard about the walk in Sydney — and became the first Australian to do it! Northallerton was the first Young Farmers' Club to complete the walk. D.W. West of Marton composed a prayer:

Thank him above for feet so trim,
And size 9 boots to put them in;
For tracks and trods that reach so far
Across the hills to Ravenscar,
Oh keep those hills as they were then,
A place for silent walking men!

J. McCarthy came up from Birmingham with a coffin and ten people in his van. He wondered just what Near Moor was near to. From mist and cloud in Bilsdale they burst into bright sunshine on Botton Head "like emerging from black and white into a colour photograph". From Loose Howe the black track on each side of the boundary stones looked depressingly like the M1 disappearing into the distance. They wondered if an elephant party had been across. They hit the waist deep bog at Fen House. Sleep-walking and in a state of utter exhaustion they reached Ravenscar at 3.20 a.m. after 20 hours' hard going.

N. Wallace, a Lancastrian, thought that Loose Howe was appropriately named. He had never seen looser ground. His party also fell into the Fen House bog. K. Lancaster's party was lost in impenetrable gloom on Carlton Moor with a thick mist dampening clothes and spirits. After hours of wandering they struck a road and phone box. They rang the operator to ask where they were but he didn't know either, so they rang the police who sent a patrol car!

M. Atkinson, Hull, did six solo unsupported crossings in 1966 and costed the operation — using motor cycle to the starting point, and buses round to collect it — at £3 4s. 3d. Using a car as support probably costs about £10, a reasonable figure of the value one might place on a crossing. On this basis the annual cash value of the Lyke Walke Walk is around £80,000 — considerably more than the total shooting rents of all the moors crossed! David Cowley (16) did a double crossing by mistake. He had walked back to Wheeldale Youth Hostel from a 7.0 p.m. finish at Ravenscar but it was closed — so he walked home!

The "youth" record has been progressively decreased. Against my advice Heather Cowley insisted on completing a crossing in October 1965, a month before she was ten. She was accompanied by Anne Walkington (12). The following year Neil Brown crossed when 7½. These youngsters seem to do it, in good company, by chattering their way across. (Now 6 years, 11 months — Christopher Turton, Bridlington).

Anne Walkington also joined in an attempt on horseback by Bill Wilson (whipper-in to the Bilsdale Hunt) and the Chief Dirger. The Army track over Fylingdales from Lownorth was followed and apart from bog near the E.W.S. and on Simon Howe all went well and we were in sight of Hamer, at the Pinkney Shooting Box, in six hours. It then took three hours to cross the next 300 yards. The trouble is a belt of peat which offers no obstacle to a man, but into which the horses sank hopelessly.

At one time we thought it might be necessary to send for a helicopter to get them out. Eventually a causeway of heather had to be built. It may be taken that the proper Classic route is impossible for horses. A way round could be found on bridle paths making a pony-trek of at least 50 miles. We are not, however, thinking of opening a horse section. I must emphasize the great danger to horses of these peat beds. We heard later of a horse being swallowed completely in a bog on Wheeldale Moor, and the bog near Loose Howe is locally called "Pannier Ass Slack" because a loaded donkey strayed off the causeway and was engulfed there.

There have, of course, been many unsuccessful attempts. Two Lancashire cyclists "more used to bikes than to boots" made one — and the mistake of steering by Venus. Also the liquid attractions of *Blakey Inn* were too strong for them, and when they re-started — still chasing Venus — their average speed was only about one mile per hour for the next six miles! By that time Venus had led them out somewhere about Stape! Another party walked steadily from the start for five hours, and found themselves in Scugdale — three miles from the starting point. They must have walked right round Black Hambleton!

A Bradford man arrived at Ravenscar to start the walk and went down with Asian 'flu. "On reaching the bar of the *Raven Hall Hotel,* I could not see straight before entering, let alone after leaving", he wrote, and he made a panic-stricken flight back to Bradford.

A London party spent eight hours getting from Hamer House to Wheeldale Lodge, and then gave it up as a bad job. J. Kane reported an interesting failure on 19th March, 1964, when they met a head-on gale and deep snowdrifts. A support car got stuck in a drift near Hamer and the occupants had to leave it, eventually getting a lift back to Teesside. The walkers found shelter in Rosedale and next day they met to dig the car out. They found another car stuck with it, whose owner turned out to be a brewery representative with plenty of free samples! Another dirger of some experience, J. Bennington, reported a disastrous November attempt from Ravenscar when with twelve others he floundered about all night and got no further than Jugger Howe! T.C. Meredith "could not get down frontwards to the stepping-stones at Wheeldale because of the pain in my knees, so I held on to the dry-stone wall and slithered backwards by gravity".

Undoubtedly the best report from a failure was by Geoffrey Newson in the *Sheffield Star* (September 7th, 1960).

There have been a succession of tall dirgers, small dirgers, slim dirgers, slow dirgers, doughty dirgers and often dirty dirgers (author's note—How true!). They have formed a Dirgers' Club, with annual dinners. There will not be a place at the table for me this year. The career of Newson, the aspiring dirger, ended on Saturday after 22¾ miles of muddy mossy moorland.

I must confess the urge to dirge has not been among my more eager ambitions. But a casual chat with R.S.M. Jack Mason, 147 Field Ambulance T.A., introduced a new word to shatter my blissful existence—dirging. In one inspired moment of pastoral enthusiasm I accepted an invitation to join in an attempt—to do a Moore on the moor. Next morning—I use the word with some euphemism, since it was 3.30 a.m.—I blundered bat-eyed from my tent.

There were several former dirgers—and Newson, a virgin dirger. Before dusk our party had produced one five times dirger (Col. Neill), three double dirgers, a new dirger—and a demi-dirger with discretion. En route to comfort we had to high step through heather like tortured Tiller girls, brush through bracken, battle through bogs, and heave over hills. Here and there we found parched piles of bones, evidently deceased dirgers of old. After 22 miles and three quarters—when the tops of my boots started chaffing my chest, I decided to accede the argument to Mother Earth.

When I die they will probably find Snod Hill written on my heart. Apart from the fact that one blistered and battered scribe missed his meal ticket for the next Club dinner, the whole operation was a great success.

Most people come back again till they do succeed, for the walk has a fatal fascination. Perhaps even Geoffrey Newson—?

Recent Years

IN the three years to the end of 1970 more people did the Lyke Wake Walk than in the previous twelve, and the grand total of crossings more than doubled, to very nearly 35,000. (Now, 1979, over 90,000).

Among groups completing the walk have been Hull and East Yorks. Institute for the Deaf; York Workshops for the Blind; S. Durham Iron and Steel Co.; British Rail Data Processing Division; The Inter-Varsity Club; Liverpool Bog Walkers; John the Baptist's Hiking Club (?); Steetley Refractories; various departments of Hawker Siddeley Aviation, Brough; 14 bottle sorters from the National Glassworks, York; the Suffolk Cragrats; the Surrey Vanguards; a Metropolitan Police party and a group of York Centenary Circuit Methodists; several Fire Brigades (off-duty); several Inland Revenue (Tax Inspection) groups (also off-duty); the Beverley Auto Club and the Hull Museums Society; a coxless eight of the Bedford Rowing Club; Bortoft's Crumpets, Manufacturers of Hot Plate Goods, wholesale only, Scarborough; the Power Gas Company and British Titan Products. There have been several international parties — Norway, Sweden, Denmark, Germany, Austria, Holland and France have been well represented — Chile, Mauritius, Poland, Sierra Leone, Finland, Fiji, Nigeria and S. Africa. There has been at least one walker each from Australia and New Zealand, and two from Wisconsin, U.S.A. Almost everyone in Hull appears to have done the walk, and even in London the Lyke Wake Club's coffin badge can frequently be met with. There is a strange story from a T.U.C. conference at Blackpool. A veteran dirger walked into one of the hotels, to be greeted warmly by the manager. "Ah, I recognise your badge, sir — we have a lot of your members here. The Undertakers' Union isn't it?"

Some 40 more people have achieved double crossings, including another woman (Hilary Clarke of Wolverhampton Mountaineering Club, a veteran vegetarian of almost 50, who did the double in 34 hours). The congregation of St. Mark's Church, Fairfield, Stockton-on-Tees, walking to raise money for a new church school, included the ten-year-old triplets, Alison, Malcolm and Howard Hammond, with nine-year-old Timothy Challands. In one international party was a Czechoslovakian who kept repeating "seventy kilometres!" in tones of stunned incredulity. Mary Wood demanded an amendment to the Divorce Bill—any man encouraging his wife to do the walk would give immediate grounds! Officers of the Royal Artillery at Bramcote have done several crossings, and their wives decided to do one with their husbands supporting for a change. The "Kitchen-sink Athletes" were getting weary by Fen Bogs and had the misfortune to get tangled up with the local hunt. They struggled up to Ellerbeck flanked by hounds with flashing fangs, apparently waiting for the weakest member to drop out. At Jugger Howe ravine the leader encouraged them with "Just a short down and up"—but as the ground suddenly opened up at their feet and full realisation dawned of what this meant, there was a Parisian protest from the French member of the party "Oh, la—you say short down and up? Oh no, this I cannot do—Eh bien, I die for France!" Another all-female party was led by Margaret Beecroft. The Department of Genetics at Leeds University ate curry at Blakey washed down with a non-vintage Medoc. They met a party of horsemen and women at Lilla Howe and felt sorely tempted to cadge a lift behind a girl with a pink blouse and bare midriff. The thought made them lose the track altogether. They suggested further research into the genetic determinants of the Lyke Wake Walk, susceptibility to doing the walk being determined by an autosomal gene L dominant in males but showing incomplete penetrance in females. The condition resembles several other inherited disorders which show decreased severity in females.

From North Wales came a Mr. Edward Howes, who found large numbers of his relatives scattered over the route—Foster Howes, Two Howes, Western Howes, Beacon Howes and so on! The proprietor of Hughes Coaches, Castleford, and one of his drivers had a go, but the driver dropped out and refused to try again till a motorway was built across. A British Railways party were dismayed to find an apparently dead walker lying near the path at Rosedale Head. As they inspected more closely he opened his eyes reluctantly, muttered "I'm all right—I've come from Ravenscar", and went back to sleep. They suggested that walkers should carry placards to place above them in such situations. "Resting—Do Not Disturb", or "R.I.P." if actually expired. Mr. T. Vickers of Leeds like many others before him had difficulty getting down the steep drop to Wheeldale Beck as his left knee was painful. The only good thing about this was that it took his mind off a sore right heel. A party from Wetherby Borstal got lost in the Derwent Valley in terribly wet conditions. Apart from three casualties (one with pneumonia) they tried again a fortnight later with success. Ian Wright of Salisbury tried in the January snow and covered eight miles in eight hours. At Easter he and a companion got to Hasty Bank before collapsing. At his third attempt he got to within three miles of Ellerbeck in August when he could stand the pain in his feet no longer and walked on barefoot. Finishing in sandals he paddled in the sea at Scarborough next day, as his feet had been strangely numb. Then he found how painful they were. He had to be carried to the Red Cross station and couldn't stand, let alone walk, for two days. John Free and Phil Balmforth of Wakefield were not reassured by arriving at Osmotherley just as a funeral procession was departing. They had an expensive prismatic compass which unfortunately enabled them to find the path from Loose Howe again just when they had lost it. "Time and distance became as nebulous as the mists around us, but at 23.00 hours John Free sank to his thighs in a bog whilst trying to avoid 6 ins. of mud on the path." With the aid of the compass they managed to take three hours to cross Wheeldale Moor, going very accurately parallel to the right path at 200 yards distance. S.W. Sands of York also reported taking a compass course over Loose Howe, and battling through deep heather "when to our delight we saw the true track to the left. Thinking the track would be easier walking we struck across to it — but reckoned without the morbid sense of humour of the Lyke Wake. Exactly at the point where we joined the track it sank into a bog and we sank with it". One schoolmaster who sank waist deep into a bog was glad because it took his mind off his feet. Another took some boys over — "the most dangerous and the most rewarding thing I have ever done. We were lost from the start as we set off in the wrong direction!"

H. Laver of York breakfasted on Carlton Bank off tomatoes, yoghurt and brown ale. After being violently sick at the Wainstones he blamed the tomatoes. John Yates of Durham finished with more blisters than toes. Vera Davies, conqueror of several long walks, finished the Lyke Wake Walk in a far dirtier condition than any of the others. J. Wigglesworth, Chartered Mechanical Engineer, of Halifax, was seized with midsummer madness on 19th June. A week later sanity had returned and only a lingering stiffness of the nether limbs remained to prove that what had happened was fact not fantasy. P.E. Smithson, of Walsall, a sedentary solicitor, thought life began at 40. But on 26th May for the aforesaid sedentary solicitor it very nearly ended on an E.-W. crossing, and there was one time climbing Cringle Moor that he seriously wished it would. H. Johnson found a body above Esklets, a dirger so exhausted that he had lain where he fell, pausing just to squeeze rucksack and transistor radio into his sleeping bag with him. Johnson murmured a brief dirge over the corpse, switched off the radio, and departed. N.A. Wilson of Saltburn had a friend who, after scrambling up Cold Moor on hands and knees, wisely became one of the support party on Clay Bank. One member of a Manchester University Polymer Research Group absent-mindedly left his trousers at the starting point. Chris Jones lost his in a Hamer bog and thereafter used a cycle cape as impromptu kilt. His party had set off across Rosedale Moor at

5 a.m. and found themselves back at the same spot at 7.30 a.m. R. Wood followed a trail of fresh orange peel and wondered if the party ahead had been sponsored by Jaffa or Outspan. Mr. J. Curry, doing his 13th crossing on Friday the 13th, remarked to Mrs. Coltman at the Pollard Café that she must see some funny sights going in. "Yes", she said quite seriously, "but they're funnier still when they try to get up to go out". Two of his boys had this conversation on Rosedale Moor: "Stop hanging on tiv us!" "But ah'm sinkin'!" "Ah knaw — but ah dinna want ti sink wi ye." D.F. Bradford and S. Sheriff took a dog across and reported by strip map with these comments:

> Dog going strong, Cringle and Cold Moors are killing us but it is the Classic route, blast it! Dog still going strong. Wainstones renamed Lamestones. Thick mist till Esklets. Dog very energetic. Weather fine from Loose Howe. Bloody dog. Clear night. Wish we were dogs. Dog going strong. Dog going fairly strong. Dog collapses at finish—now on equal terms!

Horsforth Venture Scouts commented that from Loose Howe the O.S. map shows the Lyke Wake Walk as "Undefined". They all found very good definitions for it. They crossed Wheeldale Moor in what they thought was the shallow end. Major Glazebrook, M.B.E., 1st Battn. Prince of Wales' Own Regiment, took 40 men out of 44 across:

> We leave tomorrow for Cyprus to bathe our aching feet in the Mediterranean. Our crossing was made easier by a party from Easingwold School whose superior knowledge kept us on the right path. The best description of the walk was given by my batman who did it in a pair of new experimental Army boots. Both the boots, and any attempt to repeat all he said, are doomed to failure.

Brian Wilkins and others carried a polio victim over in a chair. P. Belshaw took a party of maladjusted boys over. P.C. Devillez of Middlesex decided at Ravenscar that walking lacked sufficient entertainment and enjoyment value for him. Arthur Puckrin reported British Steel Corporation's first inter-group event over the route. Arthur had had a bad leg in the Race. At Clay Bank he discovered he had two bad legs. In the bog they had a competition to see who could find the deepest place. Arthur's experience told and he won by a thigh. Blakey Ridge at 7 a.m. was like Stockton High Street on Market Day. Flight Lt. Tait and two other R.A.F. officers after a double crossing in 38 hours wrote:

> Pain! A simple exercise in endured pain. Aching, cut and blistered feet. Creaking knees that crack and cry stop. Bits of moving skin which rub painfully against other bits that don't. Even those parts of the body that don't do anything go stiff and sore through prolonged inactivity. The terrible suffering of going downhill, the almost overpowering effort of going uphill, is only matched by the need to persuade the body to go on at all. It is worth the suffering. The pleasure of achievement; the knowledge that you can do

something which few others have the endurance to do. More important, the simplicity of it all, just walking, mixed with a little food and sleep. Escape from modern complex society to simple problems. A beautiful sunrise, desolate moorland, and tinned pineapple juice. Young grouse, flowering heather, and sitting on the edge of a stream with the water rushing between your toes. It is worth the pain. Your companions are tedious. They walk too fast or too slow. They say the wrong things or don't talk when they ought to. Suffer from different aches and problems and don't seem bothered about yours. Yet when the going is really bad one of them will always fill the gap, be cheerful when it's needed, or find the right track when you are lost. The support party. An excuse for a rest, a legitimate reason to stop, just for a moment. But they don't understand. They don't understand why you are early, or late, why you are limping or moaning, or, really, how you get from one check point to the next. But they are vital, your contact with outside, someone you can scream at without offending.

One dirger said he had followed closely in the wake of a party of nurses and doctors from North Ormesby Hospital fully confident that if anything happened to him he would be assured of expert medical attention. The further they progressed however, the less grew his confidence. The following conversation was overheard on Lilla Howe from a party nibbling Kendal Mint Cake: "It says here that Captain Scott used these on his expedition." "Look what happened to him!" "Thank God his walk never caught on!" One party leader suffered from over-exposure after climbing a barbed wire fence. Saltburn County Modern School went wrong in Raisdale, and eventually found a telephone kiosk with another party already in occupation. They recognised a Bradford accent saying, "Whoever is leading this party has as much sense of direction as a compass in an ironstone mine". They were later stopped by soldiers on an exercise who said, "You can do this sort of thing in the Army and get paid for it!" At Hamer a helicopter landed and asked if they had seen any soldiers wet and bedraggled after a night on the moor. Cheam Rover Scouts met numerous walkers, but any inquiries they made about conditions ahead brought only knowing winks and nods. The next five miles turned out to be one vast bog: "When you go in with a silent swish you know it's gonna be deep." A Hawker Siddeley party was led by two mechanical test engineers experienced in fatigue. The Petuaria Players reported in the form of a Three Act Play:

Act 2, Scene 1, Hamer—One player went stage left and found the only wet hole for miles. The unscripted "Bogger it" brought the living theatre to the moors.

Hull Multiple Sclerosis Society raised £500 by a sponsored Lyke Wake Walk. No exact account has been kept but over £50,000 has been raised for various charities on the Lyke Wake route. Ken Boaz, of Selby Round Table, suggests that the title of Drover be conferred on experienced Supporters, whose duties he defines as (1) to provide comfort and refreshment to those still mobile, (2) to offer succour and assistance to the lame and infirm and (3) to perform the last rites if and when this becomes necessary. W.S. Townson celebrated his 13th crossing entirely during the hours of darkness leaving Ravenscar at 16.30 hours on 12th December, 1970, and reaching the Trig Point at 09.08 on the 13th. George Ayre, a Ship's Pilot, reported his age to be 44 at the start, 94 at the finish—his third attempt. His feet felt as though they had been through a concrete mixer and he swore never even to speak about the Lyke Wake Walk again. "Three bashes in six weeks is drastic exercise for someone who wouldn't walk to bed if he could get the car upstairs—but I now feel fitter than I have done for many a long year. Please send me your latest leaflet for my next attempt!" Five bus drivers, four conductors, and one inspector of Hull Transport Dept. have done many crossings and include a Past Master, a Doctor of Dolefulness, and several Masters of Misery. It was suggested that we might take our own bus out to the Himalayas to do a Lyke Wake Walk across Kashmir! C.J. Charlton met two chaps doing a double. "They were whispering words of encouragement to each other, and by Jove, they needed it!"

During 1973 and 1974 there have been a dozen more double crossings, including John Scarsbrook, Denis Oglesby and Miss K. Harris. L. Kulscar did his hundredth crossing on 17th November, 1973, and Ben Hingston his on 26th October, 1974. Ian Ashley Cooper was close behind. Some 30 more Past Masters have been appointed. Thackrays of Leeds, Manufacturers of Surgical Instruments, Hospital Furniture and Sterilising Equipment, have sent many parties across. An R.A.F. party in June 1974 included Air Vice-Marshal C.G. Maughan, C.B.E., A.F.C., who completed the walk in 10 hours 55 minutes. Another joint R.A.F./R.N. party in October was led by Group Capt. D. Palmer, O.B.E. On Wheeldale one of the party thought he could see the sea but on closer inspection was dismayed to find it was Wheeldale Beck running full and wide. They found that the agony of descending to Jugger Howe ravine was only surpassed by the hell of climbing out of it. Messrs. Young, Robinson and McNalley of Reckitts, Hull, completed a crossing between sunset and sunrise on the longest night, 21st/22nd December, 1974, a feat which had in fact been done by Gene Robinson in 1971. (His time, 14 hours 38 minutes.) The Puckrins, Wanlesses, and other Lyke Wake families continue to flourish. The official W.-E. record set up by international athletes M. Turner and C. Garforth of Cambridge University in September 1970—4 hours 58 minutes 7 seconds—still stands. The last crossing of 1974 and the first of 1975 was accomplished by K. Walls and D. Taylor, who walked into the New Year. Starting at 11 p.m. and fortified by rum they completed the crossing in 18 hours but reported being passed by an older, experienced looking walker after the rum was finished (Ben Hingston).

The only discordant note was from an anonymous writer: "As a medical practitioner may I advise you strongly to see a specialist or a psycho-analyst. I know you are only an ignorant farmer but most of the ones I know are very sane ones with good feelings. If you are not ill then I advise you to go down on your knees and pray forgiveness for the wickedness you are leading others into."

During the years 1974-78, groups have come from the Knights of St. Columba; Teesside Lions; Blagdon Park Cricket Club; Whitby Lions; the Bath and West Evening Chronicle; Batchelors' Foods; Boots'; Goole Docks Social Club; Eston Rangers F.C.; Sunderland Public Works Dept.; Pocklington YFC; Lucas Aerospace; the Pilgrim School, Bedford (shades of John Bunyan!); Kossett Carpets; York Tramps; BBC Radio Ramblers; the Wellington Inn, Knaresborough; Teesside Customs and Excise; Regional Blood Transfusion Service; Woodlands Children's Home, Norwich; English Martyrs' Church, York; Cardiff and Durham Prison Staff; NALGO Pathfinders; Melton Mowbray Postmen (one double crossing here!) Reckitts Ramblers; Durham Cathedral Guild of Bellringers; Charterhouse School; the Long Distance Walkers' Association; North Sea Ferries; Heys Mineral Waters; and the Ebor Acorns — amongst very many others. There have been fifty more double crossings, including Frank Hackney and his 16 year old daughter Sylvia. Hilary Clark, vegetarian, now in her early fifties, did a second double. We think that this feat — crossing each way inside 48 hours — deserves special recognition and a specially sympathetic double-crossing card is to be instituted (and may be applied for in retrospect.) It will, of course, cost twice as much. During 1978 a group of 19 men from RAF Fylingdales made a crossing and on November 18th Ben Hingston did his 150th crossing, being now some 20 crossings ahead of Ian Ashley Cooper and Lewis Kulscar. I did a 29th crossing in September 1978 with Judy Morgan and her two daughters, Karen and Lynn. All took part in the Yorkshire TV film of the walk in winter (January 1978) which is fully reported in the new book of "Lyke Wake Lamentations". Amongst others, Eric and Margaret Toyne became Past Masters.

There have been many brilliant reports and theses (some of which appear in the new book) but space does not permit many quotations. D.I. North withheld his address in his report, wishing only to forget the walk and have nothing to remind him of the 17 hours agony he had endured. Paul Mallet found this book highly entertaining before he did the walk but whenever he looks at it now sick feelings sweep over him. J. Winkler of Oxford discovered the book on a library shelf and promptly and wisely put it back. Then a rambling club circular mentioned an annual Lyke Wake Walk so he bought the book. Another circular mentioned "highest and widest" and "adverse conditions" and his sense of adventure overcame his instinct for self-preservation. He put his name down for a walk to start June 6. On June 1 he read the book for the first time and only then did he realise the enormity of what he had undertaken! Colne Operatic Society saw a man who had started the walk with an alsatian finishing it with a dachshund. Ivor Simon, P.M., took Mark, 9.11, and Emma, 8.9, over in June 1975. In 1976 came the disastrous fires and the closure of the walk for several weeks. Walkers dropping cigarette ends in the very dry peat could have caused these fires, so please in future if you must smoke do so only at check points. In October the 21st anniversary of Walk and Club was celebrated at the Haunted Castle Hotel, Kirby Misperton, and several of the Foundation Members were present.

In April 1977 the Sheriff of York and his Lady, Councillor and Mrs Dean, were jointly sponsored for £12.50 a mile, raising £500 — it was the Sheriff's third crossing. The Mayor of Beverley, Graham Stroud, has also done several crossings — one which he led in 1978 raised £800 for charity. Barbara Mitchell crossed with husband and three children: "My toenails have gone black — is this the start of being a witch?" Mark Adlard, of Seaton Carew, drew moral support from Dante's Inferno —

"And I, staring about with eyes intent
Saw mud-stained figures in the mire beneath,
Naked, with looks of savage discontent".

He thought that John Bunyan also must have crossed Loose Howe at some time: "Now a great mist and darkness fell upon them. Here was but sorry going, the way very wearisome. Nor was there so much as one inn or victualling house, wherein to refresh the feebler sort". Dr. Robert Visick made a terrible mistake by crossing on September 9, his horoscope for which was "Good idea to keep in circulation but confine yourself to short journeys as longer ones will be too tiring." He gave bad marks to a Bradford party and a sponsored NSPCC party for dropping litter and being rude when asked to remove it. Good marks for no litter went to a Perkins party and to a grey-haired man making great speed over Fylingdales Moor picking up and burying any bottles and cans he found. Sq. Leader Hurrell A.F.C. reached the Raven Hall Hotel, but someone had to take his money to the bar for him, as having sat down he couldn't get up: "I admire your judgment in selecting just the right length for the walk. Many in the bar shared my view that if the bar had been five yards further east you'd be short of a lot of completions." Carolyn Lyness underwent the purgatorial tourification to lose weight, but found she was a pound heavier after the crossing. Two members of the Yorkshire Water Authority carried all supplies with them "but economised on water, taking only two pints each backed up with purifying tablets for topping up en route". Two thirsty Americans were driven to using water that "was a dubious orange colour with large lumps of rust — we thought the iron might be what was needed to keep us going".

Michael Dean, consultant surgeon, watched the European Games after his crossing and felt amazed that you could get a medal for a mere 100 yards dash, whilst even the marathon was only 26 miles!

Neil Blake and party thought the walk couldn't be too difficult as children and O.A.P.s did it. But starting after three hours in the Three Tuns they kept getting lost: "Our time of 23 hrs. 30 mins. may seem excessive — we only just managed it and feel that anyone else who has done so must be pretty strong characters." Yorkshire Blind Rambling Club took four completely blind members across and a boy of 8, Charles Allen. Other 8 year olds were Benedick Everett and Roger Brown. Portakabin employees sent a report "from our Special Correspondent at the front — or, more appropriately, the rear". Urra Moor had the less fit members "steaming like leaky kettles". They wished the railway was still running, and later, in Jugger Howe ravine, that their legs were of the Lodastrut variety. The support van driver had a blister on his clutch foot and £500 was raised for Cancer Research. Eleven representatives of Ladbrokes the bookmakers also walked for Cancer Research: "All were overweight and unhealthy. Of the field, four set off at a tremendous gallop and soon had a good lead, with the rest of the bunch settling in behind. The first obstacle, Live Moor, took its toll and at Hasty Bank Jimmy, the locally trained stallion, who had obviously been overworked, collapsed, as did Keith, who had too much weight to carry and was handicapped to lose anyway. Several more dropped out at the Rosedale Bend. At Shunner Howe, Dave from Redcar lost his shoes in the mire and without a blacksmith had to be retired. There were just two finishers."

Roundhay School raised £200 and thought that "never in the field of masochism have so many owed so much hell to one person." Vaughan Foster and other Malton Police Officers raised £170. St. John's, Ossett, has also raised a great deal of money for charity on the Lyke Wake Walk. Something like £100,000 has been raised so far by walkers on the route. In spite of this the Club does not feel that the Lyke Wake Walk is really a suitable one for sponsored walks, though now that the path is so well trodden the danger is much less. Could we not have some sponsored litter collection campaigns?

Two poems by G.T. Robinson [from a Thesis for the degree of Doctor of Dolefulness].

1.   *How green is Green Howe?*
       Not very green.
       All brown and dirty.
       No green's to be seen.
       Green Howe's not green.

       How flat is Flat Howe?
       Not very flat.
       Climb up from Esklets—
       You're satisfied that
       Flat Howe's not flat.

       How Loose is Loose Howe?
       Too bloody loose.
       Proof is the bog juice.
       And crucified boots.
       Loose Howe is loose.

2. A PLEA TO THE SEA

       O mighty pounding sea,
       Please do a favour for me.
       Erode those cliffs away
       At distant Robin Hood's Bay.
       Produce a new coast far
       Away from Ravenscar.
       O sea I'd love to see
       You here at Osmotherley.

(G.T. Robinson did his 26th crossing in April 1978. More of his verses appear in "Lyke Wake Lamentations", our new book of bog-side humour).

How to Reach the Starting Points

Osmotherley [West] and Ravenscar [East]

OSMOTHERLEY can be reached by bus by United (Service 289 and 295) from Teesside and Northallerton.

United (Service X99) from Liverpool to Middlesbrough passes through Manchester, Leeds, Harrogate, Northallerton, Clack Lane Ends (one mile from Osmotherley) and Stockton.

It is advisable to ring up United Automobile Services (Head Office Darlington 5252) for current services which vary between summer and winter.

RAVENSCAR is connected by bus with Scarborough (United Service 114), the services are infrequent and run on weekdays only.

The only way of leaving Ravenscar on a Sunday is by walking rather over two miles to the *Falcon Inn* on the Whitby-Scarborough road where one can pick up United Service 258 which runs between Middlesbrough, Whitby and Scarborough. The proprietor of the *Falcon Inn* asks particularly not to be disturbed by Lyke Wake walkers.

Accommodation is as difficult as public transport. The *Queen Catherine* (Osmotherley 209) has rooms but at the time of writing does not welcome walkers. Try Mrs. Walker (Osmotherley 353), and Mrs Boyes (Osmotherley 448). Mrs Coltman, Pollard Cafe, Ravenscar (Cloughton 470), has a signing-in-book and provides refreshments. Once more *please do not disturb anyone at unreasonable hours.*

Unobtrusive bivouacs may be made in many places, but not Hamer. Camp sites are available at Potto Hill, *Lion Inn,* Blakey and at *Flask Inn.* The village hall, Ravenscar, is available for large parties (Mrs. Simmons — No. 1 Station Drive).

Camping also now reported at Charles Neale's cafe, Station Square, and at Mr. White's, Bent Rigg Farm, Ravenscar.

The Lyke Wake Club

THE Lyke Wake Club must be unique in that it has no formal organisation and no subscription. It has been likened to a tribal society, the only entry into which is by ordeal! All who do the walk in the conditions laid down become members (or "Dirgers") and there are no honorary ones. The Club confines its activities to collecting information about the walk and furthering the interests of those who do the walk. It is also concerned, however, with encouraging members to learn all they can about the moors, their history and folk-lore, and to assist in safeguarding them. Circulars are issued as necessary to members who send a stock of stamped and addressed envelopes, and no reply can be sent to any communication unless a stamped and addressed envelope is enclosed. Before attempting the walk please send for the latest circulars. All who do the walk and wish to claim membership of the Club must send a full account of their walk, with details of routes and time, plus 10p (and s.a.e.) to the Chief Dirger, Potto Hill, Swainby, Northallerton. A black-edged Card of Condolence is sent in acknowledgment of successful crossings.

The Club has gradually built up, with more humour than seriousness, its own rather macabre traditions based on the Lyke Wake Dirge and other Cleveland folk-lore. The crest is a silver coffin and three silver tumuli (Ordnance Survey sign) on a black shield. The cloth badge is a silver candle and two tumuli on a black coffin. The tie is black, with silver coffins, candles and tumuli.

Women members, who may wear a black scarf with the above badge, form the Circle of Witches. Their duty is to cast suitable spells and ward off machinations of Hobs, Boggets, Gabriel Ratchets and the like. The emblem of the Club is the rowan — mountain ash, or witchen tree. This is to ward off the unsuitable spells of the witches. In explanation of some of this folk-lore see the story of the Glaisdale and Farndale Hobs, Atkinson's *Forty Years in a Moorland Parish*. There too, in Richard Blakeborough's books, and in Ford's *Reminiscences*, you will find much about the witches of this district, who so frequently turned themselves into hares, and about the ancient dialect which is still spoken in its pure form on these moors.

The Club mace, presented by Selby Round Table, is of polished rowan, with a facsimile of the Scarth Wood Survey Pillar at one end, and a coffin at the other.

From the early days of the Club a few enthusiasts used to gather at the *Queen Catherine* for what might be called a postmortem on the year's efforts. This became the Annual Winter Wake in December. As only 60 seats are available, this Wake rapidly becomes crowded out; early application is essential though the menu might frighten many away. One reporter said he would walk 40 miles to avoid it! Witches' Broth, Hare Stew with Rowan Jelly, Crab Apple Pie, and Funeral Biscuits are the tradition. The 1974 Wake was held at the *Pied Piper*, Clack Lane Ends, and the 1979 Candlemas Wake at the Village Hall, Osmotherley.

The first Midsummer Wake was held at the *Lion Inn*, Blakey, on 24th June, 1961. Subsequent ones have been at Potto Hill, where the Annual Lyke Wake Olympics are a feature (beck jumping and bog dodging championships, throwing the stone hammer, archery contest for the Potto Flint Arrow, broomstick race and best dressed witch competition).

A Black Art Gallery has been opened for which contributions are urgently requested. It is hoped to form a collection of brass rubbings as appropriate adornments for the mortuary walls. The correct dress for Wakes is of course black, but in default of this some suitable sign of mourning should be worn, and it should never be forgotten that the Wake is a solemn occasion. Any display of mirth is most unseemly, and sympathy should be indicated by deep and heart-felt groans. There should be no smoking until the loyal toast — after which churchwarden pipes may be produced. There is only the one toast, and one speech — a report, as it were *"in memoriam"*. Correspondence is referred to, such, for example, as the letter from a man who wanted to do the walk on a bicycle, and this epistle which is specially treasured:

> I have often read accounts by you and others in **The Dalesman** of the now famous Lyke Wake Walk. I am very fond of walking but have never done more than about 12 miles at a stretch. Recently I have thought I should like to undertake the Lyke Wake Walk, mainly for the pleasure it would give me in such lovely country as I understand it to be. Being that I am unfamiliar in the use of map and compass do you recommend me to do the walk alone? Also with long walks I generally find that my feet blister—water blisters and some-times blood blisters under the toe-nails. These can be very painful. Can you recommend a way of hardening the feet? Also can you please suggest any other advice—are the moors dangerous with bogs? And is that part of Yorkshire much given to thunderstorms?

For some reason this letter always reduces a Wake to tears — but, I fear, they are tears of helpless mirth rather than of sorrow.

First, however, the *"Centuries"* of the previous Wake are read by the Wretched and Erroneous Recorder. Typical *Centuries* are those of:

The Tenth Wake (being the Third Midsummer Wake, held at Potto Hill on 22nd June, 1963). The foregathering of Dirgers and Witches took place once again in the yards, barns and outbuildings constituting the Chapel of Rest of the Chief Dirger and now collectively known as the **Coff Inn.** Mourners had been arriving for the evening all afternoon and by 7 p.m. a goodly company was disporting itself in various throes of agony. The Buffet Dinner commenced at 7.55 p.m. the usual 25 minutes late and consisted of Broiled Cock Howe Cockerels on the Bone, Cringle Moor Crisps, Grilled Green Howe Sausages, Sil Howe Salad, Blue Men i' t' Moss, Simon Howe Surprise, and Bloody Beck Disaster.

At 9 o'clock the Chief Dirger prevailed upon the Miserable Mace Bearer and Horrible Hornblower to bring silence to the proceedings, which they did by adding even more noise to the existing lamentations. In the subsequent lull His Mournfulness proposed the Loyal Toast to Edward II and the Lady of the Manor of Goathland, then called for the Centuries of the last Wake to be disinterred. The funereal scribe, not having expected the solemn summons for at least another pint was buried in a tankard, and a moment or two elapsed before he and his Centuries Book could be ex-aled. The Horrible Hornblower interluded with a recital from the rafters, and ultimately the Centuries were proclaimed with due ceremony, being finally accepted without amendment. At 9.25 p.m. the Chief Dirger rose once again to present his report. His report that he had little to say this year was greeted with sombre scepticism by those assembled. Their dubiousness was indeed justified for it took His Mournfulness precisely 15 minutes to say it.

Quotations from various reports were greeted with frenzied anguish, particularly that of the pair who were in disagreement as to which direction was east. A brief glimpse of the sun proved them both to be wrong. An I.C.I. Millwrights' team split into two and disaster struck at Rosedale Head when the group with the compass disappeared over a hill top in broad daylight and were not seen again by the other party that day. The latter wandered into what they were told was Westerdale. "If our informant had not looked a bona fide local yokel, I would have called him a liar to his face." On a wet crossing two Dirgers arrived at Ellerbeck and, past caring, lay down on the parapet in pouring rain, to the consternation of passing motorists. On resuming they saw three Lilla Howes so took a mean path.

Memories of similar trials and tragedies stirred the assembled mourners, and completion of the reports evoked the usual ovation of intense woe. The Anxious Almoner was greeted with three groans of jubilation when he pronounced in triumphant misery that the Accounts were slightly solvent. A Conferring of degrees took place at 9.47 p.m., when several Masters and Doctors were engloomed in their Misery and Dolefulness. Alan Waller's Thesis for Doctorate envisaged the progressive improvement of the route by the provision of such amenities as Turkish Baths at Hamer, and Dancing Girls. The (Official) Proceedings terminated at 10 p.m.

People sometimes ask why we do not keep a closer time check of people doing the walk. For one thing, of course, it is impossible. But it is quite unnecessary. No one who attempts a walk of this kind is going to cheat. If he did, he would not last for half an hour at a Wake amongst people who know every inch of the way on every alternative route, and where details of routes and of weather are the main topic of conversation! Many people have reported failing by half a mile, some by a quarter of an hour. The challenge, and the satisfaction, are your own. It is this shared experience, of the same walk, perhaps not by quite the same route, and rarely in the same conditions, that gives a special basis of fellowship to the Lyke Wake Club. Incidentally, we are prepared to allow an extra 12 hours for every five years of age over 65!

There is perhaps no other walk which covers such a complete and well-defined stretch of hill country within the compass of one long day. So many people have done it a great many times that the Club has instituted an amusing — but none the less arduous — series of degrees. To become a Master (or Mistress) of Misery (black neck-bands) you must do three crossings, one of which must be in the opposite direction, and attend two Wakes. To become a Doctor of Dolefulness (purple bands) you must do four more crossings, one of which must be between 1st December and 28th February. You must have attended four Wakes and must present a thesis on some aspects of the walk. One more degree is that of Past Master. He must have done some 15 crossings and have contributed great services to the Club. A Past Master should be able to find his way across any moor by day or night, drunk or sober, without map or compass. The first ten P.Ms. were: the Chief Dirger, A. Puckrin, C. Bosanquet, P.A. Sherwood, J.M. Cowley, J. Adams, E. Emberton, A. Waller, Wendy Long, and Mary Hunt.

The present hierarchy of the Club is constituted as follows:

The Most Mournful the Chief Dirger [with Chief Witch].
The Melancholy Mace-bearer and the Horrible Horn-blower.
  [P. Sherwood, J.M. Cowley]
The Misguided Foundation Members.
The Cheerless Chaplain.
The Anxious Almoner. [P. Morgan]
The Sorrowful Shroud Supplier.
The Miserable Bier Carriers.
The Wretched and Erroneous Recorder (J. Scarsbrook) who
  keeps the "Centuries" of each Wake.
The Harassed Archivists —Mr and Mrs Lewis, 38 Croft Close,
  Market Weighton, York, who will be glad of any press-
  cuttings and photographs to enter in the Club's archives.
The Pro-Vice-Chancellor, P. Morgan, Chairman of the Court
  of Past Masters.
The Senile Centenarians [L. Kulscar, B. Hingston, I. Ashley
  Cooper].
The Harmonious Minstrels [E. and C. Mann, P. and M.
  Pedder].
Past Masters in order of Passing.
Doctors of Dolefulness in order of Dole.
Masters of Misery in order of Mastery.
Witches in order of Witchery.
Dirgers in order of Tribulation.

Crossings to date:

	1st Crossings	Repeat	Total	Women
1955-58 .	176	15	191	26
1959 .	89	23	112	7
1960 .	222	33	255	15
1961 .	650	150	800	35
1962 .	1,100	267	1,367	
1963 .	1,054	409	1,463	
1964 .	1,413	592	2,005	
1965 .	2,042	771	2,813	
1966 .	2,537	723	3,260	
1967 .	3,434	1,059	4,493	
1968 .	4,795	1,235	6,030	
1969 .	4,513	1,286	5,799	
1970 .	5,008	1,166	6,174	
1971 .	5,458	824	6,282	
1972 .	4,546	669	5,215	
1973 .	5,809	467	6,276	
1974 .	6,301	405	6,706	
1975 .	7,829	370	8,199	
1976 (fires)	4,794	377	5,171	
1977 .	7,917	421	8,338	
1978 .	9,353	587	9,940	
Total to date	79,040	11,849	90,889	

A check on east-west crossings revealed only 507 in 1967 as against 3,986 west-east. About 6% of crossings are by women.

Access to the Moors

UNTIL recently there has been no question of any limit of access to the open moorlands of North-East Yorkshire. Since early boyhood I have been accustomed, like many others, to walking with complete freedom everywhere. In nearly 40 years there is no moor I have not crossed and I have never met anything but natural obstacles. The National Park Acts might have been expected to make such free access more certain, but such has not been the effect.

In 1955 the Lyke Wake Walk went across open country and uninhabited moor from end to end. Since then have come the Early Warning Station on Fylingdales; forestry and fencing in Wheeldale Gill, in Bilsdale and Scugdale, and all along the scarp of the Cleveland Hills; the bulldozing of firebreaks or access roads on some of the finest moors; the Glider establishment on Carlton Bank; and the Bilsdale TV mast.

Some landowners have expressed their desire to keep walkers off open moor and have succeeded in excluding from the Rights of Way map some footpaths which were undoubtedly ancient ones, though little used in recent years. On their side it may be said that such paths were never intended for the urban civilisation which now is ours, and that large numbers of walkers do indeed cause disturbance to grouse and sheep. When the rent of a grouse moor can be based on well over £3 a brace, considerable financial loss can be caused to landowners by constant traffic in the wrong place.

With the numbers involved on the Lyke Wake Walk we have always sought to compromise and take full account of the interest of both landowners and walkers, and we hope all who attempt the walk will honour our agreements.

On the wider issues of access it may be argued that while due regard should always be paid to the needs of agriculture, and shooting is a recreation for some as well as an important source of revenue for others, the priority use of all open moor and mountain should be for recreation for the many. This land more than any belongs in the last resort to the people of England. Most of it is still as it has been for three thousand years. The Lordship over vast tracts of it was given thoughtlessly away by medieval rulers, or has been purchased cheaply in more recent times, but always subject to

85

common rights of grazing and turbary. More than one landlord has lately enclosed for forestry sections of hillside and moor where ancient rights of common existed but are not now used. Villagers whose grandfathers had the right to cut peat and bracken there are not even allowed to wander off the public footpath.

For the public at large there appears to be no legal redress. There is no common law right for the public to stray over an open space. But under the National Parks Act the local planning authority can make access orders or agreements, and must pay compensation to landowners where financial loss is proved. This seems the proper way to approach the problem — not to quarrel with landowners, but to press for implementation of the National Parks Act.

During 1978 a National Park/Landowners/Walkers Working Party has drawn up a Linear Access Agreement which may shortly be implemented. At times of great fire risk the Walk may, as in the past, be closed temporarily. Unless the moors as a whole were closed, careful scrutiny of this book, and the O.S. maps, would suggest alternatives but the Club would only approve of these in special circumstances.

The Lyke Wake Walk has sometimes been criticised for attracting so many for the first time to the beauty of the high moors and the fascination of crossing them by day and by night, in all weathers. A minority, like a minority of motorists, misbehave. Most who come for the challenge become real lovers of the moors, of which the Lyke Wake Club exhorts all its members to take proper care. Any negative attitude to this type of walk is regrettable. It is foolish to complain of the younger generation and yet limit in any way the few opportunities for adventure and exploration in wild places that still exist. That over eight thousand young people every year are prepared to complete the arduous 40 miles of the Lyke Wake Walk is something to be proud of. These and many more will come to this and other "open country" walks whatevery difficulties are placed in their way. But with goodwill on all sides the good far outweighs the harm.

Conditions

1. The walk, suggested by Mr W. Cowley in *The Dalesman*, August 1955, is the complete traverse of the North Yorkshire Moors at their highest and widest part, in 24 hours.
2. Start from Triangulation Pillar 983 (982 on recent maps) Grid Ref. 459997, on Scarth Wood Moor, and finish at Ravenscar, classically at Hotel bar, but pylon near Beacon Howe will be accepted. The *Raven Hall Hotel* and bar are closed during the winter as well as the Hotel itself. Food and accommodation cannot be relied on in Ravenscar unless ordered in advance. Lyke Wake cars must not use the private road to the TV station at Osmotherly. To avoid disturbance to farms the walk may now start at the car park near the reservoir below Scarth Wood Moor. Please do not make any noise in Ravenscar or Osmotherley at night.
3. Route must cross Stokesley-Helmsley road between Point 842 (Clay Bank Top) and Point 503 (Orterley Lane End), one mile south of Chop Gate; the Whitby-Pickering road between Point 945 (north of Sil Howe Quarries) and Point 701 (north of Saltersgate); the Whitby-Scarborough road between Point 538 (south of Evan Howe) and Point 579 (the *Falcon Inn*).
4. Route must stick to the tops as far as possible. (Parties going via Egton-Grosmont have been disqualified).
5. Before doing walk, send stamped and addressed envelope for latest information to Potto Hill, Swainby, Northallerton.
6. Full report of walk, details of route and times, should be sent to Chief Dirger. Enclose s.a.e. and 10p per head for Card of Condolence. Do not disturb anyone at unreasonable hours. Telephone enquiries should only be necessary in an emergency.
7. *Please* take care to keep the moors tidy. Carry away any litter you bring with you. Collect and bury any you find.
   In dry weather do not smoke or use matches near heather.

NOTES:
1. A narrower definition of the Lyke Wake Walk as the "Classic" route first laid down, with only one or two alternative sections, is now generally followed.
   The total amount of climbing on this is about 5,000 ft.
2. A ski crossing in 24 hours *daylight* will be accepted.

STORM LONGING

Come, friends of my heart, to the hills we'll fly,
   Where the high winds never rest,
But storm and cry on the Riggs that lie
   To the eastward crest on crest;
Where rain and sleet in tempest beat
   Round many an ancient Cross,
From Crookstaff Hill to Wheeldale Gill,
   From Bloworth to Yarlsey Moss.
When the sea-roke spread on Botton Head
   Rolls down to the dale beneath,
And our way we thread with careful tread
   Through the gloom of the trackless heath;
When the sea-wind snarls from Stony Marls
   And the sky's a leaden cloud
That hides the brow of Shunner Howe
   Like a Norseman's funeral shroud.
But what reck we of roke or storm
   Or the furies overhead?
A song we'll sing as on we swing
   With sure and steady tread.
Though boggets growl and ratchets howl
   As we tramp on side by side,
Through the night that's black with storm and wrack
   Our steps the gods shall guide.

(1935)